# All About Horses

# All About Horses

Sue Allfrey

WARD LOCK LIMITED·LONDON

**Acknowledgments**
The publishers would like to thank the following for
supplying extra pictures for the book:
Sue Allfrey pages 44, 46 and 48; Australian Information
Service, London page 22; British Tourist Authority pages
8, 53, 69, 80 and 83; Canadian High Commission,
London page 86; Colorsport pages 9, 55, 56, 88 top and
below and 92; Gerry Cranham page 90; Kit Houghton
page 60; Keystone pages 10 and 81 top; Leslie Lane pages
27 and 28; Pictor pages 40 and 81 below; Picturepoint
page 33; Peter Roberts page 47; Keith Stevens page 58;
Sally Ann Thompson/Animal Photography pages 12, 15,
19, 66 and 72; John Topham pages 36 and 62; Chris
Walker page 85.

*Frontispiece*: **Heavy horse with
traditional decoration of raffia
rosettes and bells, taking part in a
folk festival in the Netherlands.**

Illustrations © Ward Lock and Uitgeverij Het Spectrum B. V.
De Meern, The Netherlands 1980, 1986.

Text © Ward Lock Limited 1986.

First published in Great Britain in 1986
by Ward Lock Limited, 8 Clifford Street,
London WIX IRB, an Egmont Company.

Designed by Heather Sherratt
Text filmset in 11 point Palatino
by Preface Ltd., Salisbury, Wilts

Printed and bound in Czechoslovakia

**British Library Cataloguing in Publication Data**

Allfrey, Sue
  All about horses.
  1. Horses—Juvenile literature
  I. Title
  636.1    SF302
  ISBN 0-7063-6299-3

# Contents

# Evolution of the horse

The horse we know today has developed from a small animal about the size of a fox, with four toes on his feet, who roamed the world about sixty million years ago. The evolution of the horse is a remarkable example of how an animal adapts itself to a changing environment and way of life. The need for increased speed was the main reason for adapting; to achieve this the animal needed to get up on tip-toe, which meant the weight had to be carried on its inner toes. Over millions of years the outer toes lost their use and finally disappeared until the horse's hoof developed as we know it today.

Wild horses inhabited Europe up to the end of the nineteenth century, but today there is only one species of wild horse in existence, the Mongolian Wild Horse, better known as Przewalski's Horse. This breed is pale dun, has a large head, and is now confined to the Gobi Desert, apart from zoos.

The various environments, climates and conditions in which horses have developed have led to the different types of horse that we have today. Broadly speaking, there are two main groups of domestic horses, the northern or cold-blooded group, which derived from the heavy pre-historic horse of central Europe, and the southern or hot-blooded group. Interbreeding has produced what is usually referred to as the warm-blooded group.

Pictures of man mounted on horseback date back to 2000 BC but it is known that horses were driven before they were ridden; so we can assume that man has been making use of the horse for at least 4000 years.

When horses were first bred domestically, they were used for milk and meat. When the nomadic tribes found that horses could be used as pack-animals they began to breed them for work as well.

Horses were used for hunting by the Persians, Egyptians and Assyrians several hundred years before Christ. They drove them in chariots and later rode them across country after gazelle and wild boar. Hunting in Britain has always been considered the sport of kings, and is well illustrated by many accounts in our history books. A greater cross-section of people enjoy hunting today than ever before, but it still has royal patronage, although today the wild boar has been replaced by the fox.

The first war-horses were of stunted pony size, and were used to convey the warriors by chariot. Many centuries were spent trying to develop a larger and stronger animal which would be suitable to carry a warrior clad in armour on its back; it is from the war-horses

*Opposite*: A pair of Dutch Draught Horses drawing a wagon delivering lager in Amsterdam. This breed was developed from Belgian, Brabant and Ardennes heavy horses.

7

of the Middle Ages that many of our heavy horses are derived today. Most armies of the world relied totally on horses for transport until the beginning of this century; they were not finally disbanded from the British army until 1969. Thousands of horses have been involved and killed in every war and campaign up to the Second World War. Today military horses are confined to the more peaceful duties of the parade ground.

Racing was known in Syria and Arabia many centuries BC. The Greeks and Romans became expert horsemen, and racing soon became as popular as chariot races in the Olympic Games. The Romans introduced horse racing to Britain, but it was not until the reign of James I that public races became established. James I was responsible for introducing Arab blood to his stud, and, among other horses, imported the Markham Arabian. Charles II also imported oriental horses, many of whom appear in the pedigrees of horses in the General Stud Book.

The importation of Arabian stallions continued during the early part of the eighteenth century, and it was during that time that three stallions of particular importance arrived in England. It is from these three stallions, the Darley and Godolphin Arabians and the Byerley Turk, that all modern Thoroughbreds descend in the male line.

Racing, too, has always been the sport of kings; even today there are few monarchs who do not support racing or own racehorses.

The horse has been man's main form of transport since it was first domesticated, firstly as a pack-horse, then driven with a crude form of cart and later ridden. The Roman Empire depended on pack-trains for its commerce and in England during the 1690's a regular pack-horse goods service ran between Exeter and London.

Members of the King's Troop, Royal Horse Artillery, whose duties include ceremonial parades, and performing musical drives at horse shows, where spectacular speed and precision in manoeuvring the very heavy gun carriages is essential.

The first private coaches were cumbersome and uncomfortable; and it was not until the invention of springs in the beginning of the eighteenth century that people began to travel by coach rather than on horseback.

The mail service relied on horse transport until the introduction of railways. The Pony Express in America had relays of riders who galloped across the country. In Britain the mail was carried by top-booted horsemen who were restricted to a speed of 7 mph (11.3 kph), until the introduction of the mail-coach services, in 1786.

Horse-drawn covered wagons made it possible for the settlers in America, South Africa and Australia to open up their vast countries and establish communications. In every country in the world horses have provided transport for man since he first learned to drive and ride them.

The horse has also played a very important part in agriculture, although today the vast combine harvesters and other equipment of

The Grand National, Aintree, Liverpool, the most historical and spectacular steeplechase, with the biggest public following. At 4 miles 856 yards it is the longest and has the most fences – thirty of them, all faced with gorse.

9

A Gaucho (mounted herdsman) at work on an estancia (cattle farm): Entre Rios, Argentina.

the prairies leave little room for the heavy horse. In Europe, they may still be seen, most frequently used for horticulture; a horse will walk carefully between rows of vegetables or fruit bushes, where a tractor cannot be taken.

Entertainment is still a field in which the horse excels. Apart from the race track, horses nowadays form the main attraction at shows throughout the world, where show jumping has become a 'big business' sport. Horses used for bullfighting are superbly trained and cared for, unlike the pathetic horses used by the *piccaloes* years ago.

The liberty horse of the circus, although not so common as it once used to be, may still be seen in the larger circuses, as may the heavier type of horse used as rosinbacks for the acrobatic displays. No Western show would be complete without the rodeo, where today's cowboys test their skills against their companions in the many and varied competitions.

The Lipizzaners used by the Spanish Riding School in Vienna have for centuries, thrilled their audiences with performances of *haute école*, and are probably among the best-known horses in the world.

## The Arab

The Arab, the oldest of all recognized breeds of horse, has had more influence on horses the world over than any other breed.

Arabian people were pictured with horses more than 700 years BC, but it may well be that the Persians were breeding these horses before that time. Horse pedigree records date from the sixth century AD; horse breeding has been an important part of the lives of the desert Bedouin since then.

Today the Arab horse is bred all over the world; the danger facing his future is that his great popularity could result in careless over-breeding, with the production of inferior stock, lacking the true Arabian characteristics. Arab blood has the capacity to mix with almost any other and to improve the resulting stock. All horses in competitive sport have Arab blood somewhere in their history, the Thoroughbred having descended directly from the Arab.

King Hussein of Jordan, anxious to preserve the true desert Arab, has been carefully breeding these horses at the Royal Stud since 1961. He has now built up some truly magnificent stock with indisputable ancestry and beauty.

Britain imported Arabs several centuries ago. Those of greatest consequence were imported during the first half of the eighteenth century. Some excellent studs have been built up; of most historic interest is the Crabbet Park Stud, where Wilfred Scawen Blunt and his wife Lady Anne Blunt bought stock direct from the tribes of the

A pair-horse sleigh. Bells worn on the harness signal its approach. Sleighs are widely used in winter for recreation and transport to places inaccessible to motor vehicles.

11

An Arab mare. Britain imported Arabs several centuries ago and they have been used to improve the quality of Thoroughbreds and some native breeds.

Arabian desert, to found the famous stud in Sussex. By 1909, ninety-six stallions were standing at stud there. Great interest was awakened in the breed, and since then Arab studs have been developed all over the world.

Much has been written about good and bad points of Arab horses. One indisputable fact is that they are regarded as the most magnificent of all horses. The head should be very short and refined, with the characteristic 'dished' face; the muzzle exceptionally small and soft, the nostrils large and elastic, so that they can flare out with excitement. The eyes are large and dark; they should be set wide apart and are lower in the head than in other horses. The jaw is rounder, and set wide apart, so that a clenched fist fits between the jaw-bones. The ears, set well apart, are small, well defined and alert.

The neck must have a distinctive arched curve, formed by the angle at which the head and the neck join. This feature is peculiar to the Arab, and determines the amount of movement of the head. The mane and tail hair, also a distinguishing feature, must be fine, silky and soft.

The chest must be broad, the shoulder sloped and long, joining the neck, which should be long enough to give a good length of rein, with the short, slightly concave back. The loins are particularly strong, the croup wide and level and the tail is set on high. The bone structure of the Arab differs from other horses, as it has fewer ribs and lumbar bones. A good Arab should have extreme length from hip to buttock and the gaskins should be strong and prominent.

The bone of the Arab has greater density than any other breed; the limbs are strong and clean with well-defined tendons. The knees are flat, the cannon bones short, the pasterns set at a good angle leading to near-perfect feet, any fault in these being regarded most seriously. Although the hindleg is not the strongest point of the breed, good Arabs are straight in the hindleg, the hocks set low to the ground and following the line of the leg.

The 'floating' action of the Arab is one of the most distinctive characteristics of the breed. They must have great freedom of movement at all paces, and appear as though they are moving on springs. The trot, with little or no knee action, must be full, free and generous, without the exaggerated daisy-cutting action that predominates in show classes.

## The Thoroughbred

The development of the Thoroughbred has been the greatest contribution that Britain has made to the horse world. The fastest and most valuable horses on earth, they are used world-wide for racing.

All Thoroughbreds can be traced through the male line to the three Arab horses that were imported about the beginning of the eighteenth century – the Byerley Turk, and the Darley and Godolphin Arabians. Horses had been raced in Britain since Roman times, but it was not until the now extinct, native Galloway pony was crossed with imported oriental blood that the Thoroughbred as we know it today began to evolve. With racing much encouraged by Charles II, breeding suitable horses became important, and several noteworthy studs were formed.

In 1791, the first Weatherby's General Stud Book was published, by which time a definite pattern of selective breeding had been established. The word Thoroughbred (a literal translation of the Arabic 'kehilan' meaning 'pure bred all through') was not used until 1821; and it was much later that the English Thoroughbred became established as a breed.

The development of the racehorse in other countries was never so successful as in Britain. This resulted in the export from Britain of much good Thoroughbred stock. From such small beginnings, only 250 years ago, there must now be nearly half-a-million racehorses throughout the world all having descended from the three Arab stallions originally imported to Britain; to say nothing of the millions of part-bred horses used in competitive riding.

The Thoroughbred has been bred for his speed. The action must be long, free and easy, enabling him to cover as much ground as possible with each stride. A good sloping shoulder, plenty of depth

Horses bunched closely as they round a bend during a flat race. Some jockeys are wearing goggles to protect their eyes from flying mud thrown up in the soft going.

through the girth, combined with powerful quarters and hindlegs, are essential. Many Thoroughbreds inherit the slightly dish face, small neat ears, and the fire and courage of the Arab.

Generations of systematic breeding for speed have, however, resulted in a loss of much of the inherent soundness that is a characteristic of the Arab horse. The racing of Thoroughbreds as two-year-olds, before they have had time to develop and mature, must be largely to blame for this situation. The constant carrying of weight at speed must inevitably throw an unnatural strain on their immature structure, resulting in much wastage.

Although an excellent ride, Thoroughbreds do need expert handling and are not suitable for weekend hacking. There can be few more sorry sights than a retired racehorse who has fallen into the hands of someone lacking knowledge; and is seen in a bleak paddock in wintertime, huddled under a hedge for protection.

The Thoroughbred has been bred for speed and is used world-wide for racing.

Racehorses need to be stabled and looked after by experts; they have for generations been bred to be the finest of all horses, and their treatment should be of the best.

## The Hunter

The hunter is a type of horse and not a breed. A hunter can be said to be a horse that is suitable for carrying a person to hounds. They originated in the British Isles where hunting has been and still is a large part of the tradition of the country people.

The English hunter normally has Thoroughbred blood in its veins; in some areas pure Thoroughbreds make excellent hunters. A hunter must be capable of carrying his rider over a variety of terrain, at various paces, and negotiating any obstacles that come in the way. He must have stamina to be able to 'stay' all day and cover anything up to 30 or 40 miles (48–64 km) if required. Soundness is a vital ingredient, as an unsound horse can be the ruination of a good season's hunting. A good, comfortable ride is also essential. A horse that jars its rider on every stride will not only be uncomfortable, but also extremely exhausting to ride all day.

For obvious reasons there must be numerous types of horses that are all suitable for hunting. The type of country will greatly influence the stamp of horse that is most suitable. The open galloping areas of the 'shires' will need a big bold horse, able to go at a good gallop. The hill areas of Wales will need a short-coupled

15

cobby type of animal, able to negotiate trappy, awkward fences. The weight of the rider will also be of great importance; a lightweight teenager will want a totally different horse to a large well-built man.

In the show ring, hunters are normally divided into three groups according to weight-carrying ability: lightweights who are judged suitable to carry up to 12½ stone (79 kg), middleweights up to 14 stone (88 kg) and heavyweights over 14 stone. There are also classes for small hunters who must not stand more than 15.2 hands high.

Ireland must be mentioned when discussing hunters. Traditionally a horse-breeding country, Ireland has not only produced some of the best racehorses ever seen, but also many excellent hunters. The Dublin Horse Show, the most famous in the world as far as hunters are concerned, is renowned as a 'shop window' by thousands of hunting enthusiasts. It is a five-day show held in August, on the Royal Dublin Society Ground. Many of the best hunter-type horses have been bought in Ireland for other sports, notably show jumping and eventing, and they have made names for themselves in national teams.

Many heavyweight hunters have been produced by using a Thoroughbred stallion on an Irish Draught mare; the danger at the moment is that so much Thoroughbred blood has been used to give quality to hunters that the genuine weight-carrier is in danger of disappearing.

When judging hunters the judge must assess the conformation, ride, movement and manners. Conformation in the hunter is of great importance as this will influence soundness, movement and ride.

In the USA horses are expected to show their jumping ability in the show ring. In Britain the more recently introduced working hunter classes fulfil this requirement, and are becoming very much more popular.

## The Hack

As with the hunter, the hack is a type of horse as opposed to a breed. The name 'hack' is essentially British and of quite ancient origin. Today hacks are rarely seen other than in the showgrounds, but a century ago that was not the case. A hack can be used to describe any horses used for leisure riding. However, having said that, the type of horse used a hundred years ago is the stamp that is still sought after by the judge of hacks today.

There used to be two types of hack; one was the Covert hack, an animal on which the owner rode to the meet; meanwhile his hunters were hacked on by grooms, and he changed on to one of these to follow hounds.

There was also the Park hack, a more elegant and refined animal, on which the owner, attired in the height of fashion, used to indulge in a little gentle exercise. Ladies, riding side-saddle, and gentlemen, usually in morning dress, rode for leisure in their parks at home, or in the public parks in towns, such as Rotten Row in Hyde Park. The Park hack was therefore required to look very elegant, move beautifully and have impeccable manners.

These are all the qualities still sought after today. The ideal hack must have excellent conformation, a small refined head, graceful neck, good sloping shoulder with rather pronounced withers, short back and powerful quarters. The legs must be clean and strong and the movement straight, true and level. Most hacks today have a high proportion of Thoroughbred in them, although small hacks often have some pony blood as well.

Show classes are usually divided into two sizes; large hacks who must not stand more than 15.3 hh and small hacks that do not exceed 15 hh. The show hack must be both a pleasure to behold and to ride. Producing a hack is a very specialized art, for although a horse may have the looks and movement of a champion, unless his manners are perfect and he is a delight to ride he will not be a winner. Whilst being expected to be capable of galloping, the canter of a hack should be almost as slow as the walk, a feat requiring a high degree of schooling.

Although there are exceptions to the rule, in general hacks do not make good dressage horses, as was once supposed; the requirements, apart from complete obedience, being very different. Renewed interest in hacks has once more established them in the horse scene, where hopefully they will remain a joy to behold and to ride.

# The Cob

The cob, like the hunter and the hack, is not a breed but a 'type' of horse. The most important quality of a cob is that it must be an animal with 'weight-carrying' ability.

Cobs were frequently dual-purpose horses, used as much in harness as under saddle, for which they were ideally suited. With the introduction of motorized transport, the popularity of the cob declined, but today it is once again becoming recognized as a useful riding animal.

A cob should be a short-legged, stocky animal, the height limit being 15.1 hh. He should have a quality head set on an elegantly arched neck, the back should be short, the girth deep and the quarters and second thigh well muscled and powerful.

A cob should be a comfortable ride, well-balanced whilst active. He must be able to gallop and jump but must not 'hot-up'; he must also be 'handy' and have good manners. They make ideal mounts for elderly people, being easier to mount and more reliable than high-couraged hunters. Cobs are also ideal for young people who have grown out of ponies but who do not have the experience to handle a 'blood' horse.

There is no particular blood line to follow to breed a cob; most are produced by chance, as the result of mating different types of animal.

Needless to say, many of the best cobs are seen in the show ring. It was traditional to hog cobs' manes and to dock their tails to emphasize their stocky appearance. Since the practice of docking was made illegal in Britain in 1948 this practice has been dropped, although most cobs are shown with their manes hogged.

# *Riding horses of the world*

## The Americas

American history has been greatly influenced by the horse. It was on his back that armies travelled, conquests were made; that different cultures and civilizations met and mingled. He has been used for transport in quests for new territory and has been valued as a friend and companion. Horses of Spanish origin were the first to be introduced to the American continent, by Hernando Cortes when he set out to conquer Mexico in 1519. These, with subsequent importations from Britain, Europe and the East have been the basis from which the great herds of 'wild horses' developed and also from which the recognized breeds we know today have derived.

### Quarter Horse

The Quarter Horse is the best known of the American horses; he is regularly exported abroad, particularly to Australia where his fine qualities are much coveted. The breed has a long history dating back to colonial days when horses descending from the original Spanish stock were crossed with blood horses imported from England. The most famous of these was a grandson of the Godolphin Arabian, named Janus, who is considered the ancient foundation sire of the present Quarter Horse breed.

Virginia and the Carolinas were the home of this breed, where they were used by the cowboys in their task of cattle herding. A favourite Sunday pastime was holding match races between owners of their fastest horses. These were held down the main streets of towns, few of which had a street more than a quarter of a mile (.4 km) long, and from this these stocky fast-starting little horses took their name. Selective breeding has produced the fastest horse on earth over a quarter of a mile, but it is not speed alone that makes him so popular; his equable disposition, being easy to handle, combined with intelligence, superb conformation and agility make him widely sought after.

The average Quarter Horse stands between 14.3 and 15.1 hh; he is a rather stocky horse, with short-coupled but very strong back, especially across the loins. The neck is of medium length, well-muscled but not too heavily crested, and carries the distinctive head fairly high. The head should be short with a small muzzle, foxy ears and well-developed jaw. The chest is wide and deep,

A Quarterhorse stallion, showing the well-developed quarters which help to make it so strong and agile. Chestnut is the predominant colour of the breed.

allowing plenty of heart room, but without coarseness. The hindquarters are broad and heavy with powerful muscles, especially in the thigh and the gaskin, and the stifle is wider than the hips. It is from these tremendously powerful hindquarters that the Quarter Horse gets his quick acceleration and ability to stop rapidly; it is these assets, together with an inborn cow-sense and agility that make him supreme in the many fields in which he competes. The lighter types often sired by a Thoroughbred are used for racing, while the more stocky types are frequently seen at rodeos where they excel in events such as roping, reining, cutting and barrel racing.

**Morgan**

The Morgan breed all descend from one horse, a colt given to Justin Morgan, an innkeeper, in payment of a debt in 1793. He was essentially a working horse, used for the clearing of land for homesteads, but earned his owner money from match-racing, weight-pulling contests and as a trotter in harness. He so excelled in these contests that he was in great demand as a sire. Most breeds evolve over several generations, but with the Morgan it happened in only one generation. The phenomenal feature about this tough little stallion was that, no matter what sort of mare he mated, it was his own fine qualities and looks that he passed on to his offspring. He lived to the ripe old age of thirty-two and stamped all his progeny the same way, so that well before his death the breed had become established.

The Morgan was used primarily as a working and saddle horse. During the time that tram-cars relied on horses Morgans were in great demand in New York because of their great pulling power.

The average Morgan stands between 14 and 15 hh, bay being the predominant colour. The proud head is small with neat ears and a

19

large expressive eye. The shoulder is well-sloped, the back short, the barrel deep and rounded and the loins strong. The main and tail are thick, the tail being carried high.

The Morgan has largely influenced the formation of three other American breeds, the Standardbred (*see* Chapter 6), the Saddlebred and the Tennessee Walking Horse.

**The Saddlebred**
This was developed to suit the requirements of the settlers who developed Kentucky. Larger than the other breeds, standing 15.2 to 16.2 hh, this elegant horse derived from the crossings of Thoroughbreds, Morgans, Standardbreds and Carolinian Naragansett Pacers.

They were originally used for general farm and saddle work; however, their good looks and ability to perform at five distinct smooth gaits brought them into the show world. As a result of intensive breeding to enhance the best of gait and conformation, the Saddlebred is today used almost exclusively for the show ring or pleasure riding. The high head carriage and action are definite handicaps when jumping.

The refined, rather narrow head, with large wide-set eyes is carried on an elegant long neck, running into a fairly high wither. The well-sloped shoulder, short-coupled back, level croup and rounded quarters, give strength and thrust to the smooth gaits. The limbs are long and fine with well-defined tendons. The mane and tail are of a silky texture and very fine. Rich coppery chestnut is the predominant colour, but bays, blacks and greys are quite common, and more recently a number of Palominos have been registered.

**Tennessee Walking Horse**
One of the more recent, but very distinctive breeds to have been developed in America, is the Walking Horse. This horse was developed by the plantation owners, who had to spend hours in the saddle, seeing to their estates, and wanted a horse with particularly smooth gaits.

The breed evolved from crosses of Standardbred, Thoroughbred, Morgan and Saddlebred. Their average height ranges from 15.2 to 16 hh; larger than most other breeds, they are full of substance although very compact. Both the head and neck are rather long, the head being held high with narrow pointed ears. A sloping shoulder is essential to give the smooth ride required, the back being extremely short while the quarters slope slightly. An abundant tail is carried very high. The legs are fine, the forelegs set well forward while the hind legs are set with the hocks well away from the body.

The gaits of the Walking Horse are unique to the breed; they are completely devoid of jarring and are all developed for comfort. The flat foot walk is a true four-beat gait in which the horse seems to glide over the ground; the running walk is a much faster version where the hind legs overstride the front legs and the head shows a pronounced nodding. The canter is a very distinctive movement where the horse elevates his forehead in a forward rolling motion while the hind legs continue in a trot-like movement.

The Walking Horse is rarely used on plantations these days.

Show horses are usually trained and produced by professionals, while others are used for pleasure and are usually owner-trained and ridden.

Other breeds in America have also derived from the original Spanish and British imports.

The Mustang developed directly from the original Spanish imports that escaped and lived wild; spreading from Mexico up to the Canadian border huge herds of 'wild horses' established themselves. With no selective breeding, these 'wild horses' inevitably lost some of their grace and size, but developed into very tough, intelligent and alert little horses. The Indians, realizing the value of the horse, soon equipped themselves with large numbers of these 'wild horses', many of which were coloured.

The Appaloosa, now recognized as a breed, was originally bred by the Nez Percé Indians as a war-horse. By careful crossing with Quarter Horses they have been developed into eye-catching stock horses. Their coats are spotted, either with dark spots on a light coat, or the reverse.

The Paint and Pinto horses are both coloured horses, and both have their own breed associations. The Paint horse is very similar to the Quarter Horse and is used as a stock horse and in rodeos for roping, reining and calf cutting etc. A registered horse must be sired by a registered Paint horse, Quarter Horse or Thoroughbred.

Pintos include horses of all breeds; they were very popular with the Indians because of their built-in camouflage. These horses fall into two types; the Tobiano which is basically white with large patches of colour; and the Overo which is a dark coloured horse with white splashes.

The Palomino and Albino also have their own associations, but these are essentially concerned with colour and not specific breeds.

## Australia

Horses were first introduced into Australia in the eighteenth century. With the introduction of cattle and sheep, horses became very necessary to tend the herds and flocks on the vast open plains. Horses of Dutch, Spanish and Arab origin from South Africa were the first to be imported; later these were mixed with Thoroughbreds.

### Walers

Named after New South Wales, Walers developed from these imports; they are hardy little horses, standing 15 to 15.2 hh. They are close coupled with a good sloping shoulder and length of rein. They have very good limbs and feet, are speedy and long-striding with a deep chest, plenty of heart-room and exceptional stamina.

The American Quarter Horse has been introduced over the past few decades, and very successfully crossed with the Waler. However when it comes to galloping fast over long distances after cattle in the heavily-timbered bush, the Australian cowboys still prefer the Waler.

### Brumbies

During the days of the Gold Rushes, horse breeding was neglected and horses roamed the range, breeding at will. These horses are known as Brumbies; they are very tough and wily and difficult to catch. Hard-riding 'Brumby runners' made their living from driving these horses into cunningly concealed stockyards and then capturing and selling the best of them.

Unfortunately these horses are now considered of little use, and their numbers are being reduced by slaughter for pet food.

Racing is one of the most enthusiastically supported forms of sport in Australia. 'Picnic races' take place in the outback, where the amateur riders, usually local stockmen, race their horses on a dusty bushland track. There are now a number of high-class studs where the breeding of top-quality Thoroughbreds is an important industry. Nearly all Thoroughbred stock is descended from horses imported from Britain, but more recently first-class stallions have been imported from France and the USA.

Flat races predominate in Australia. Despite the firm going, some steeplechases are included in the programme at Melbourne Racecourse, home of the celebrated Melbourne Cup. This takes place each autumn, when thousands of enthusiasts flock to the racecourse from all over the country.

Arabian horses have become very popular in Australia; they are mostly used for pleasure riding and have been most successful in

Horses parade round the paddock before the race at Morphetville, Adelaide, South Australia.

endurance contests. They are also seen in the colourful costume classes at shows, where the riders dress up in Bedouin costume. Most Arabs have been imported from Britain, but blood from the USA has also been used more recently.

Many breeds of British native ponies are to be found in Australia, the Welsh and Welsh Mountain ponies being two of the most popular. The Shetland and more recently the Connemara have been in demand. Hackney horses and ponies have been exhibited at shows for many years, as have the heavy horses, the most popular of which is the Clydesdale.

## Austria

Horses have played an important part in Austrian history. They are still the centre of attention at the most famous of all equestrian centres, the Spanish Riding School in Vienna. The most important breed today is the magnificent Lipizzaner.

### Lipizzaner

The Lipizzaner must be one of the best known breeds in the world, made famous by the magnificent stallions used in the Spanish Riding School in Vienna (*see* Chapter 8).

The breed was founded at Lipizza, from whence it takes its name, in 1580 by the Archduke Charles II. He was responsible for importing nine Spanish stallions and twenty-four mares, which formed the basis of the future breed. Later there were additions of Italian, German and Danish blood. In 1717, a stallion of Spanish origin, called Lipp, was purchased; his descendants proved to be some of the best stud horses for over a century. Later oriental blood was introduced, one of the most famous being an Arab stallion named Siglavy, who came to the stud in 1816. He is one of the six blood lines to whom all Lipizzaners can still be traced today.

The present-day Lipizzaner usually stands between 15 and 16 hh, although some smaller and larger ones are used in the riding school in Vienna. They are nearly always grey; the foals are born dark but get paler with each change of coat, until they achieve the characteristic whiteness associated with the breed by the time they are seven to ten years old.

Lipizzaners are bred for the Spanish Riding School at its stud at Piber, near Graz, Austria, founded in 1798. After weaning the foals are branded for easy identification.

The letter 'L' for Lipizzaner is put on the left cheek, the stud brand, a 'P' for Piber, surmounted by the Austrian Imperial Crown is put on the left croup, the ancestral brand, denoting the stallion line of both parents under the saddle on the left side, while on the right side, under the saddle, the number of the foal is placed. In this way all Lipizzaners bred at one of the official studs may be recognized, and their breeding traced.

Lipizzaners are docile horses, strong, durable, very teachable, intelligent and well behaved. The head often shows some Arab influence and the neck is set high and carried nobly. The strong back is muscular and ends in a very powerful croup. The tail is set high and is thick and silky, the limbs compact and clean with well formed hooves. They are one of the slowest horses in the world to mature, but compensate by living to a great age. Stallions that are used in the Spanish Riding School in Vienna as school horses may serve for twenty or twenty-five years, several of them living till thirty or more.

## France

### Camargue

The Camargue area in the Rhone delta in the south of France is the home of the Camargue horses. These small tough white horses come from a very ancient breed that descended from the pre-historic horse of Solutré. What is certain is that in spite of crossings down the generations, mostly with Barbs, these horses have maintained their hardiness.

They are known as the 'white horses of the sea', although the foals are normally born dark; the coat changes to the characteristic whiteness, like the Lipizzaner's. Camargue horses live in the marshy delta area, surviving on a diet of tough grass and salt water. One of the few breeds that still live wild in herds, there are probably between 400 and 500 Camargue horses today.

They stand between 14 and 15 hands high. Their conformation tends to be poor; they have large square heads, short necks and

'White horses of the sea'. There are about thirty herds of Camargue horses living around the Rhône delta of France.

upright shoulders. However, they do have short strong backs, a good depth of girth and plenty of bone with good hard feet.

They are ridden by 'gardians', the local cowboys who use them for herding the famous black bulls of that area, which are seen in the bullrings. The ponies are noted for their ability to twist and turn and to gallop, all very essential to the tending of wild cattle.

### The French Anglo-Arab

Anglo-Arab means a mixture of Thorough and Arab blood, but in France it has a special significance. Although Anglo-Arabs originated in Britain (the breed society is the Arab Horse Society), they are bred in many other countries. Napoleon Bonaparte showed a preference for Eastern-type horses. Soon after this, during the mid-nineteenth century, many English Thoroughbreds were imported from Britain for racing and these were crossed with mares with a lot of Arab blood; this breeding has continued till the present day. To qualify for the French Anglo-Arab register a horse must have at least 25 per cent Arab blood.

They make excellent riding horses, usually combining the best qualities of both breeds; the speed and substance of the Thoroughbred with the natural balance, agility, pride of bearing and good temperament of the Arab.

Measuring anything from 14.3 to 16.2 hands high or more, the French Anglo-Arab has proved itself an excellent saddle horse, excelling in racing, show jumping, dressage, hunting and eventing. Usually bay or chestnut, the head is delicate, the nose straight, the eyes set wide and expressive. The well-set neck joins a good sloping shoulder, the back is short and the quarters long and flat. The limbs are sound and although the bone may be light below the knee, it is very dense, allowing these horses to carry plenty of weight.

### Selle Français

The Selle Français is a very recent breed of horse, which has been recognized as a breed since 1965. The name simply means French Saddle Horse.

These horses stand between 15.2 and 16.3 hands high and are strong, of good conformation, ideally suited to competitive riding, show jumping and eventing. Any colour is permissible; chestnut is predominant.

# Germany

In Germany the emphasis in horse breeding has been placed on power and a temperament that can stand the extreme discipline demanded by German riders. Breeding is not controlled by the state, as in Sweden, but is supported by provincial organizations, the breeds mainly being defined by the birthplace; thus horses born around Hanover are registered in the Hanoverian Stud Book; this has resulted in a loss of distinction between breeds. The exception is the Trakehner, which originated in East Prussia. Three of the most important breeds are the Hanoverian, the Holstein and the Trakehner.

### Hanoverian

The best known of the German breeds, the Hanoverian as we know it today is a comparatively recent breed. It owes its origin to the influence of the British Hanoverian kings, who took a great interest in breeding a really good all-round horse, suitable for riding, driving and draught work. George I sent many British Thoroughbreds to Germany to cross with the local mares; and George II founded a stud at Landgustüt at Celle in 1735, where Hanoverian stallions are still trained.

Recently breeders have concentrated on producing a lighter, more elegant saddle horse. British Thoroughbreds and Trakehners have been used to upgrade the horse and give him more courage and stamina. Hanoverians are big upstanding horses, with good conformation, excellent limbs and powerful quarters, standing 16–17 hh. They are very active and bold, with the courage but not the speed of the Thoroughbred. All solid colours are acceptable, most being bay, brown, chestnut or black.

Hanoverians are exceptional movers, with equable temperaments, which makes them most suitable as top class dressage horses and show-jumpers.

### Holstein

Holstein horses trace back to the fourteenth-century war-horse. Additions of Spanish and Eastern blood made them lighter; then in the nineteenth century they were improved by the use of Cleveland Bay and Yorkshire Coach Horse stallions. The Holstein has always been a big strong horse, used as a coach horse and for the artillery of the army. It has less Thoroughbred blood than most other German breeds, so tends to be heavier than the Hanoverian.

The lighter horses have been developed for riding horses, using Thoroughbred blood to improve them; they are all-round saddle horses, many of them making excellent show jumpers. The average height is 15.3–16.2 hh, the usual colours are bay, brown, black, with many greys being used as coach horses. Holsteins are powerfully built, with strong quarters, a good depth of girth and plenty of bone. They have good shoulders but are inclined to be rather short and thick in the neck. They are willing to work, intelligent and good-tempered, which make them easy horses to handle.

### Trakehner

King Friedrich Wilhelm I founded the stud of Trakehner in 1732 in the north-western part of East Prussia. For more than 200 years the tradition of breeding horses flourished, for the cavalry as well as for private use, until the stud was destroyed at the end of the Second World War.

Much Arab blood was used during the early days of the stud; later British Thoroughbreds were extensively used, until by the First World War 80 per cent of the mares were by Thoroughbred stallions.

When the Germans retreated from Poland at the end of the Second World War, they took 1,200 Trakehner horses with them to Germany, and their progeny established the breed in Germany as it is now.

Here, Swiss World Champion dressage rider Christine Stückelberger rides Granat, a pure-bred Holstein, at the 1976 Olympics in Montreal, where they won a gold medal.

Today there is no national stud, but the Trakehner is bred privately throughout Germany. They are excellent saddle horses, frequently making top-class jumpers. Much of the Thoroughbred influence can be seen in them; standing 16.0–16.2 hh, they have excellent conformation, any solid colour being acceptable. They are kind horses, but still retain the lively spirit of the Thoroughbred and the great stamina for which their ancestors were noted.

## Ireland

For hundreds of years Ireland has been noted for the many fine horses it produces, more than ever since the Second World War when improved transport has assisted buyers and sellers alike in promoting horses bred in Ireland.

The horse is rooted very deep in Irish tradition, most farmers still keeping a mare or two for breeding purposes. With this enormous

27

wealth of horse flesh it is rather surprising to find that Ireland can only claim two noted specific breeds, the Irish Draught Horse and the Connemara pony.

Irish Thoroughbreds have been exported throughout the world, claiming immense influence on racing both in Europe and North America. The favourable conditions in Ireland are the mild climate and the limestone qualities in the water, which with the fertile pastures help young horses develop good bone and substance. As a result numerous studs have been developed, producing many of the classic winners throughout the world.

The majority of horses apart from the many racehorses produced, are a mixture of Thoroughbred and Irish Draught, producing many excellent horses of hunter type, several of which have become famous in the sphere of show jumping and eventing.

**The Irish Draught**

A light draught horse, this breed probably derived from the Connemara pony, and developed in size when reared on the excellent grasslands of southern Ireland. A general-purpose farm horse that was also a good traveller on the roads, the Irish Draught has proved an excellent producer of high-class heavyweight hunters when crossed with the Thoroughbred.

A parade of young Irish Draught Horses at the Dublin Horse Show. Their breeding is encouraged by the Irish Horse Board. Crossed with a Thoroughbred, the Irish Draught produces excellent hunters and eventers.

Standing 15–17 hh, the best have excellent shoulders, good neck and head carriage and a free and easy action. They have good sound legs with only a very little hair on the fetlocks, the usual colours being grey, bay, brown and chestnut. Most are naturally excellent jumpers, their progeny frequently making top-class show jumpers.

The breed was drastically depleted during the First World War when large numbers were acquired by the army, who found that with so little hair on their legs they did not suffer from 'greasy heels'.

Their numbers were also sadly reduced by the export of mares to the continent for meat. It was not until the mid 1960's that legislation was passed to stop this trade, since when there has been an increase in the number of registered mares.

# New Zealand

Horses in New Zealand come mainly from Australia, but somewhat different types have been developed to suit the varying interests.

The Thoroughbred is extensively bred and raced; many people think that the cooler climate and resultant good grazing provide a better environment than in Australia. The Arab too is very popular; introduced from India in the 1920's, there are now several large and important studs.

Hunting is a thriving sport in the Islands; excellent hunters are bred; they tend to have more Thoroughbred blood than British hunters, and are trained to jump wire.

In the Lake Taupo district, large herds of wild horses thrive, belonging to the Maoris. They stand about 14.2 hh, are a mixture of various bloods, including Thoroughbred, and make excellent cow ponies.

# Spain

Spanish horses can rightly claim to have had a great influence on many other breeds of horses. The most important, the Andalusian, came from the region of Andalusia in the south of Spain. When Hernando Cortes led a handful of riders to overthrow the Aztecs and capture Mexico for Spain, he proclaimed 'After God, we owed our victory to the horses.' These were the first horses taken to America, and formed the foundation on which all American breeds are based. The Lipizzaner also owes its foundation to the Andalusian and many other European breeds have been improved by the introduction of Andalusian blood.

### Andalusian
The Andalusian is one of the oldest breeds in Europe. They originated when the native Iberian horses were crossed with Barbs brought in during the Moorish invasion.

The Andalusian is a strong active horse with enormous presence, combining agility and fire with a docile temperament.

For centuries artists and sculptors have used horses of

Andalusian type as their model for important works of art; an example is the mounted statue of King Charles I in Trafalgar Square.

The Andalusian has retained the Barb head, with large, kind well-set eyes, a broad forehead and well-placed ears. The neck is quite long, and well-crested in the stallion, the well-defined withers join the short back, from which he derives his agility, with the powerful quarters. The croup is gently rounded, neither flat as in the Arab, nor steeply sloped like the Quarter Horse. The shoulder is long and sloping and the chest broad. The legs are clean cut and elegant, yet robust enough to withstand the great demands placed on them during the work required.

Usually white, grey or bay, the Andalusian stands about 15.2 hh. For centuries they were the most sought-after horses in Europe; at one time a ban was placed on the export of breeding stock for fear of the breed not being maintained.

Many of these are highly trained in *haute école*, being used during the parades preceding bullfights, when they may be seen performing several *haute école* movements, one after the other.

# USSR

Russia may well have been where horses were first domesticated; certainly the oldest of all known breeds, Przewalski's Horse, still exists in its wild state on the eastern frontier.

The Soviet government's horse breeding policy is probably the envy of most other countries. With such a variety of terrain and extensive distances, the government has tried to encourage the development of two or three breeds in each zone. There are now forty breeds in Russia, some of them developed during this century, others imported, but most of them long established.

Horses are evaluated between the ages of two and four years old and are then classified into different standards. Only those in the best group will be selected for use as stallions, although most of Russia's horses are kept entire.

### The Akhal-Teke

The Akhal-Teke is a very old breed, skeletons of similar horses having been found from over two and a half thousand years ago. Associated with the Turkmenian people, the Akhal-Teke has been much influenced by Arab blood and probably developed from Turkmene horses. They are noted for their incredible endurance and are ideal horses for desert conditions. Some took part in a famous trek in 1935 from Ashkabad to Moscow, a distance of over 4,100 km (2,500 miles) which included 360 km (225 miles) of desert; this was covered in only three days by these remarkable horses who travelled without water.

The Akhal-Tekes are small distinctive horses; they stand between 14.2–15.2 hh and have a long lean appearance. The head and neck are quite long, as are the body and legs; the shoulder is sloping and the tail set on low. Their manes and tails are very fine and sparse. A distinctive feature is their unusual colouring; whilst some bays and greys occur, the majority are pale chestnut, the coat having an unusual metallic sheen, either golden or silver which looks amazingly beautiful in the sunlight.

The unusual methods of horse management in the central Asian deserts, where the horses are kept tethered and under blankets, may account for the uncertain temper of this breed. However once co-operation has been obtained they do make good all-round saddle horses, some of which excel at racing, whilst others excel in dressage.

## The Budyonny

Named after a Russian cavalry general, Marshal Budyonny, this breed developed between 1920 and 1950 as cavalry mounts by crossing Don mares with Thoroughbred stallions. Very careful selection of the best progeny were then interbred, their offspring being tested on the racecourse and for riding. Only the best of these were then used to create the Budyonny breed.

Still bred in the Rostov region where it originated, the Budyonny is a horse of excellent conformation standing 15.2–16.0 hh. The attractive head is carried on a long elegant neck, the body is strong and has good depth, the legs are strong, well-proportioned and have good bone. Their temperament is calm and sensible, which combined with their good looks and stamina, make them ideal for competition work.

Budyonnys have proved themselves in many endurance tests, and have won many steeplechases, including the gruelling Pardubice, which is a marathon steeplechase race in Czechoslovakia.

The predominant colour is chestnut, though bays and greys are common. Like many other Russian horses, they usually have the metallic bloom to their coats that makes them stand out from other horses.

## The Don

The Don horse was used by the Don Cossacks as early as the eighteenth century. It was riding these amazingly tough horses that the Cossacks marched on Paris in 1812, harassing Napoleon's ill-fated army, then back across Europe into Russia again.

Various strains of Turkmene and Karabakh blood were introduced by allowing captured stallions to run with the Don herds which were kept on the vast Steppe pastures. In the nineteenth century some English Thoroughbred and Strelets Arab stallions were used, but since the beginning of the century no outside blood has been introduced.

Hundreds of years on the steppes, foraging for themselves during harsh winters, has made the Dons very tough horses that are used to fending for themselves. They make ideal mounts for herdsmen, and have proved themselves in both long distance rides and for racing. In 1951 the stallion Zenith established a record by covering 311.6 kilometres (193½ miles) in twenty-four hours (twenty hours of action with four hours rest).

Dons are wiry horses, rather long in the leg, standing 15.1–15.3 hh. The predominant colour is chestnut, with the characteristic golden sheen, with bays and greys also occurring.

# Heavy horses and their work

Heavy horses have been developed over many centuries in different parts of the world, but mainly in Asia and Europe. In Britain heavy horses were imported in the fourteenth century; crossed with native stock, they provided the heavy horses used for war.

In later years, as man learnt how to cultivate the land, horses were used to provide the power for all forms of agricultural work. When motor transport became established in the 1920's, there continued to be a demand for dray horses to work in towns.

Horse trading was big and profitable business. The horses were bred, reared and broken on the farms. An experienced horseman was able to work an in-foal mare until the day before she foaled, and many a time a mare could be seen in light work with her foal trotting along beside her. The foal was weaned at six months and grown on for eighteen months. Most horses were broken when they were rising two, during the early months of the year when there was less work on the farm. Progress was made slowly, only a little being done at each session, patience being essential. The young horses were introduced to a bridle and taught to move from one side of the stall to the other by word of mouth. They were taught to trot in circles in both directions, something that would prove useful in later life. When they had learnt to respond to pressure put on the bit, a pair of plough strings would be attached to the bridle and they would be driven between the strings, as one does when long-reining a horse. After several outings in this fashion a collar would be fitted and a pair of traces. These would later be attached to a tree trunk, and the young horse would learn to feel the weight this exerted on the collar and become accustomed to the sensation of pulling a weight.

These two-year-olds would then be left to develop physically for another year and then begin their work as three-year-olds. The second stage of their training was to work beside an old horse on the plough. Two hours of work a day was enough to begin, this being gradually increased to half a day. During the next two years a young cart-horse would learn to do many different jobs on the farm; then by the time he was a five-year-old, he would be ready to be sold on and would very likely be sent by train to one of the towns where he would spend the rest of his working life.

During the nineteenth and early part of the twentieth century, apart from the transport provided by rail and canal, practically everything was moved by horse power. In many parts of the

*Opposite*: Bay Shire gelding at the Royal Windsor Horse Show, driven to a solid-tyre dray owned by Courage Brewery. The groom is there to help in an emergency and to hold the horse's head when it halts. The apron and bowler hat are the traditional dress for driving heavy horses.

European continent horses are still used extensively in agriculture, for there are many places where a tractor cannot go. In horticulture they are frequently used in preference to a tractor as they do not pan down the ground with wheel marks and can walk between rows of plants sown closely together.

Some breweries still find it more economical to make town deliveries by horse-drawn drays rather than by lorries. These prove a great attraction at many of the agricultural shows where they can be seen in all their splendid harness.

Heavy horses have been exported all over the world. Australia imported many horses until the outbreak of the Second World War; their numbers dwindled rapidly with the development of agricultural machinery but the Clydesdale has survived the best, their numbers being on the increase again.

The USA also imported, and still imports, many heavy horses, mostly British. Heavy horses are still used for farming by the Amish people in Pennsylvania. There are several heavy horse auctions each year, the biggest being at Waverly, Iowa.

Great enthusiasm is shown over the teams of heavy horses displayed by the breweries. One firm has two teams of eight-horse hitches almost constantly on the road; these are Clydesdales and are regularly seen at the big shows and in commercials. In Canada a brewery has an eight-horse team of Belgian horses in constant demand.

The most important breeds of heavy horses are briefly described here, the majority of them European in origin.

## Austria

The heavy horse still plays a very important role in Austria, where there are three times as many registered heavy horse stallions as there are warm-blooded stallions.

### The Noriker

This horse takes its name from the state of Noricum and is otherwise known as the South German Cold Blood. This is one of the oldest breeds of heavy horse in existence and is probably descended from the native Haflinger ponies with other blood introduced to increase the size. These horses stand 16.0–16.2 hh; they are sturdy with short legs and pasterns and are very sure-footed. The heavy head is set on a short, thick neck; the back is rather long. The stallions all undergo careful selection to prove willingness in harness, the ability to pull a heavy load and to walk 500 metres (547 yards) and trot 1 km ($\frac{3}{8}$ mile) in a given time. Predominant colours are bay and chestnut, the breed being found throughout south Germany as well as in Austria.

## Belgium

Belgian heavy horses have for centuries been recognized for their courage combined with power and speed in action. They have been used extensively by other countries to improve or establish new breeds of heavy horse, particularly in France and Germany.

In spite of mechanization, horses are still used extensively in agriculture where there are still about 80,000 working, although there are very few used in industry.

### The Ardennes
The oldest of the heavy breeds in Belgium, from which several other breeds have descended, the Ardennes was mentioned by Caesar as a hard and untiring working horse. Napoleon also praised them during the war in 1812, when they proved to be the only horses capable of dragging his artillery across difficult country.

The modern Ardennes has been influenced by the Belgian Draught Horse. A stocky horse standing 15.1 to 15.3 hh, the usual colours are sorrel, roan, bay and chestnut. They are economical feeders and are noted for their kind temperament but lively disposition. They are particularly suited to work in the hilly districts like the Ardennes and in Sweden, which now breeds its own type of Swedish Ardennes.

### The Brabant
In spite of importations of lightweight horses from other countries, the Belgians have faithfully kept their lines of heavy horses and have established themselves as excellent breeders. Brabant horses have exceptional utility and great draught-powers; the breed first became known as the Flanders Horse but more recently was named the Brabant. There are three main groups in this breed, each established by a famous sire. They are massive and powerful horses standing 16.1 to 16.3 hh, thick-set, stocky and close to the ground. The legs are short and strong with much feather, the chest broad, croup well-muscled, but the head is proportionately small.

# Britain

Heavy horses have been part of the British scene for many centuries. In 1310 Edward II first imported Lombardy horses from France, which were crossed with native breeds to produce the war-horses used in the Middle Ages when knights rode into battle on their chargers.

Later these horses were bred in great numbers, when transport and agriculture relied entirely on horse power. As mechanization was introduced, the need for heavy horses diminished, and the breed was in danger of extinction. Today there is renewed interest in heavy horses, many of which are exported, particularly to North and South America. The three British native heavy horse breeds are the Clydesdale, the Shire and the Suffolk Punch.

The Percheron was introduced from France during the First World War, since when it has been extensively bred and used.

### The Clydesdale
The most northerly British breed, this horse developed round the Clyde valley in Scotland. It was originally used for carrying; with

the coming of the Industrial Revolution, a heavier horse was needed, to be used for transporting coal from the mines as well as agriculture. The local mares were crossed with heavier Flemish stallions to produce the Clydesdale that we know today.

Similar to the Shire horse, the Clydesdale is a little smaller, standing between 16 and 17 hh and somewhat lighter in build. The usual colours are bay and brown, although there are both greys and blacks. They have an abundance of 'feather' on their legs and usually much white which may extend to the belly. They are very active horses and must have a high-stepping, springy action. Great importance is placed on sound legs and particularly feet, which must be open and round. The Clydesdale combines great stamina with strength and an amenable disposition, making it an easy horse to manage.

**The Shire**
One of the oldest breeds, the Shire horse has descended from the medieval war-horses. As their name implies, they originated in the 'Shires' (Leicestershire, Staffordshire and Derbyshire) and were developed for use in agriculture and to pull great weights. The Shire Horse Society was formed in 1878, since when careful records have been kept.

A Shire mare and foal turned out in traditional style for the show ring. Some of the decorations help to keep flies away; the bells on the mare's martingale warn of her approach, and were often put on heavy horses for this purpose.

The Shire is one of the largest breeds in the world, the stallions sometimes standing over 18 hh and weighing over a ton (1 tonne). They may be bay, brown, black or grey, the legs carrying much 'feather' which is frequently white up to the knees and hocks. These large, powerful horses, which can easily pull five tons (5 tonnes), have a big barrel with powerful, well-muscled necks, shoulders and quarters. In spite of their immense size, they are very docile and easy to manage.

### The Suffolk or Suffolk Punch

As its name suggests, the Suffolk Punch originated in Suffolk but it has, for many generations, been widely used throughout East Anglia. The breed can be traced as far back as 1506, one interesting feature being that every horse can be traced through the male line to a horse foaled in 1760.

The Suffolk stands about 16.2 hh, rather smaller than the Shire, but weighs as much, many being over a ton (1 tonne). Unlike the other heavy horses, the Suffolk has clean legs with little or no 'feather' and must be one of seven shades of chestnut with few white markings. It is barrel-bodied with rather large head and great depth of neck in the collar. The legs are well-muscled with short cannon bones and up to 11 ins (28 cm) of bone below the knee. The Suffolk has great qualities of stamina combined with power; it is unusually long-lived and can thrive under poor feeding conditions.

# France

The French have maintained a horse breeding policy since 1665, when Colbert involved the French Sovereign officially in horse breeding activities. About 2,000 national stallions are maintained, their upkeep being part of the national budget. France has more breeds of heavy horse than any other country and they are still widely used by farmers throughout the regions.

### The Ardennais

Originating in the French Ardennes, in Lorraine and in Champagne, this stocky, compact horse is the most popular heavy horse throughout France. The severe climate in the winter restricted the size of these animals, who rarely obtained a height of more than 15 hh. However, the introduction of Belgian blood after the Second World War has increased the size up to 15.3 hh. In their native area most horses are kept stabled throughout the winter, being put out to grass in the spring.

The Ardennais has a massive bone structure with short, stocky legs and is well-muscled. Its docile nature and gentleness account for much of its popularity, together with its adaptability to all types of farm work. The most usual colours are bay, roan and chestnut.

### The Boulonnais

These horses come from the border country on the north coast of France and are descendants of the ancient north European heavy horse. They have infusions of original blood dating from the Roman invasions of Britain, Arab blood during the crusades, and Andalusian blood, much of which is Arab. Although they have become heavy horses standing between 16 and 16.3 hh, they have retained much of the oriental elegance and intelligence. They have a short head, straight or concave nose, small ears and mouth with a fine skin and silky coat. Easy to confuse with the Percheron, they are more majestic and must be grey, bay or chestnut.

### The Breton

Three types of Breton developed in its native region of Brittany; a light type of carriage or saddle horse that is now almost extinct; the Postier Breton which was crossed with the Norfolk Trotter and used as a coach or light draught horse; and a heavy draught horse. These horses are exceptionally hardy and have great qualities of endurance and liveliness. They stand about 16 hh, have a rather concave, expressive head, strong arched neck with a short wide body and muscular limbs. Usual colours are red and blue roan, chestnut and bay.

### The Percheron

Originating in the Perche region, an area of fertile hills west of the Parisian basin and the south of western Normandy, only horses born in the region are eligible for registration in the stud book. Several other breeds have derived from the Percheron but each of these has its own stud book. Oriental blood traces back to Napoleon's grey Arab chargers, although more recent crosses of heavy horses have increased the size of the modern heavy horse so that it stands 16 to 17 hh.

The Percheron has a strongly built frame but has retained many of the qualities of its Arab ancestors. It has a sloping shoulder like a riding horse and a pointed chest with prominent breast-bone. Its wide body allows it to cover a great amount of ground without appearing too big. For an animal weighing up to a ton (1 tonne) it moves in remarkable harmony and balance. These horses are more highly strung than most heavy horses and need careful handling to obtain the excellent results in their work of which they are capable.

Usually grey in colour, although there are some blacks, the Percheron was exported to Britain in 1916 where it rapidly became popular. It was crossed with the Thoroughbred to produce heavyweight hunters, which accounts for the great number of grey heavyweight hunters seen around. It has also been exported and become popular in Canada, the USA and Argentina.

# Germany

### The Rhenish-German Cold Blood

At the beginning of this century this breed was numerically the largest in Germany. The increased agriculture and industrialization caused a great demand for heavy draught horses. Based on Belgian horses with some importation of British Clydesdales and Suffolks, this breed was developed in the Rheinland and, after the First World War, became recognized as the Rheinisch-Deutsches Pferd

(Rheinish-German Horse). In Westphalia a heavy type of horse was preferred, but in other areas a medium-sized animal was most popular and it is these that have survived the best. Belgian stallions were used to maintain the type who were noted for their early maturity, good temper and economical food conversion. The change to mechanization brought a decline in their popularity and their numbers have now dwindled to the extent that only a few are produced each year in some small areas.

# Hungary

Hungary has been famous for its horses for centuries, producing many outstanding horses which were much in demand in other countries. Although Hungary is most noted for its riding horses, particularly Arabs, there are also several breeds of heavy horse.

**The Murakosi**
This breed originated in the region of the Mura river from which it takes its name. It is one of the more recent breeds, having been developed during this century. The foundation mares were a local type; Percheron, Belgian, Ardennes and quality Hungarian stallions were used to improve the breed.

There was a great demand for these fast-moving quality horses who were capable of heavy agricultural work. By 1925 more than 20 per cent of all horses in Hungary were Murakosis and the breed went from strength to strength until the Second World War when it became sadly depleted.

After the war, Ardennes stallions were imported from France and Belgium and the breed soon became re-established. It is classed as cold blood but many of these horses are of excellent quality. The breed now has two types: a heavier one standing 16 hh or more; and a smaller, lighter type. The most usual colours are bay, black and chestnut; there are also greys and roans.

**The Nonius**
This breed was founded on one stallion, Nonius Senior, who was captured by the Hungarian cavalry from the Rosières Stud near Nancy, in France, at the beginning of the nineteenth century. He produced fifteen outstanding stallions from a wide variety of mares. The breed developed until 1890 and the registered descendants of Nonius included 2,800 stallions and more than 3,200 mares.

They are excellent dual-purpose horses used for a wide variety of work, from sporting to light agricultural tasks. When mated with Thoroughbred stallions, Nonius mares produce excellent hunters and show jumpers. The usual colours are black or brown, the height varying from 14.2 to 16 hh.

# Italy

There are three main breeds of draught horse in Italy; in addition there are about 1,000 Belgian heavy draught horses.

## The Avelignese

This is a small dual-purpose breed standing between 13.3 and 14.3 hh, used mainly as a pack-horse in the mountains but also for light agricultural work. It is very like the Austrian Haflinger, to whom it is related, both having descended from the now extinct Avellinum-Haflinger. The Avelignese has a short, somewhat heavy neck, short legs and powerful quarters and great strength for its size. Its colouring is similar to the Haflinger: chestnut with flaxen mane and tail, sometimes with white face markings.

## The Italian Heavy Draught Horse

The most popular heavy horse in Italy, this horse is bred for meat as well as agricultural work. It is most common in the region around Venice and throughout northern and central Italy. Standing between 15.0 and 16.0 hh, this very dark liver chestnut horse is noted for its speed in action despite its very heavy build.

## The Murgese Horse

The Murge district of Italy was noted for its horse breeding for centuries but about 200 years ago, it nearly died out. The present-day Murgese horse is a dual-purpose horse used for light draught work and as a saddle horse. Crossed with warm-blooded stallions, some outstanding riding horses have been produced. They stand between 15.0 and 16.0 hh and are nearly always deep chestnut in colour.

# Switzerland

Horses play an important part in the life of Switzerland. Many parts of the country are not accessible by mechanized transport and here the horse has proved invaluable. The government has been active in encouraging the breeding of suitable animals and buys horses for the Infantry Supply Columns.

### Franches-Montagnes

Three-quarters of Switzerland's horses are light draught horses of the Franches-Montagnes breed also known as Freiberger or Jura. It originated a century ago by crossing native mares with Anglo-Norman stallions and possibly introducing other blood, but has been kept pure for a long time now.

Standing a little over 15 hh, these horses are very compact and immensely strong and active. They proved invaluable to the Swiss Army during both World Wars and are still used for draught purposes. They are also extensively used for agriculture, being ideally suited to the numerous small family farms in the less accessible regions.

# USSR

The Central Soviet Government encourages the horse breeding programme of each of the fifteen republics and, to improve the

*Opposite*: Farm horses in Hungary. These are a light versatile type, suitable for riding as well as light harness work.

agricultural horse, the state maintains stallions of the most popular breeds at state breeding farms. There are several breeds of heavy horse in the USSR, which are smaller than their British counterparts but are used extensively in agriculture and horticulture.

### The Lithuanian Heavy Draught Horse

This breed originated from crossing Zhmud horses with various breeds to increase the size, the Swedish Ardennes proving the most effective. Selective breeding of the best cross-breds to produce strong, good-natured agricultural horses resulted in the Lithuanian Heavy Horse which became officially registered in 1963.

These impressive looking horses with massive shoulder and neck muscles have a long, broad body with relatively short but powerful legs. They stand about 15.2 to 16 hh and are mostly chestnut in colour. They have great pulling power and are frequently winners in pulling competitions in the Soviet Union.

### The Russian Heavy Draught Horse

This breed was founded, mostly in the Ukraine, in the latter half of the nineteenth century. Local cart-horse mares were crossed with Ardennes and Percheron stallions and some Orlov Trotters. The intention was to develop a hardy but powerful horse who was required to work fast. This was achieved within a few generations and Russian Heavy Draught Horses won several awards at the Paris Exhibition in 1900. These horses stand about 14.2 to 15 hh and are usually chestnut or liver chestnut. They are energetic and active and noted for their good nature; it is claimed that a team of three once pulled a vehicle containing seventy people!

### The Soviet Heavy Draught Horse

This is the most popular breed of agricultural horse in the USSR. Like the other breeds described, it has evolved by crossing local mares with imported stallions; in this case with Belgian Brabants, Ardennes and Percherons. Selective breeding of the best crosses during the latter part of the nineteenth and the early twentieth centuries resulted in the breed being registered in 1940.

Standing about 16 hh, these horses are rather similar in type but larger than the Lithuanian Heavy Draught. They have a longish body, strong, powerful legs and well-developed muscular system. They are energetic and tend to be lighter in build than most European heavy horses, also better suited to the climate.

### The Vladimir Heavy Draught Horse

As with the other Russian breeds of heavy horse, the Vladimir has developed by crossing local stock with imported stock, in this case Clydesdales and Shires. This has produced the largest of the Russian heavy horses, standing a little over 16 hh. Breeding was started in 1886 and during the next forty years sufficient cross-bred horses had been obtained to breed selectively from them to retain their best qualities, the breed becoming recognized in 1950.

This breed retains many of the Shire's characteristics; usually bay, often with massive white 'feather', these horses combine great pulling power with adequate speed in action.

**Dairy horse farming**

For so long heavy horses have been associated with farm and draught work that to imagine them as milk producers is not easy. Nevertheless, that is exactly what they are being used for in some parts of Asian USSR to the south and south east of the Ural Mountains.

The practice of milking horses varies in scale; sometimes it is seasonal with peak production in early summer. On other farms, several hundred mares are kept and milking operates throughout the year. Russian and Soviet breeds are mainly used; they have a docile temperament and are easy to handle. They are run in large groups in simple housing and utilize cheap bulk foods such as silage. The foals mature early, reaching 70 per cent of their adult weight by the time they are a year old. This is an indication of the high milk production of their mothers, where lactations in excess of 5,000 litres (1100 gallons) of milk are recorded.

With selective breeding for milk, no doubt the length of the lactations will be increased as well as the total output. It has been found that the mares let their milk down best when a foal is standing alongside. Special machines have been developed and the milking is carried out in a heated parlour during the winter. The mares are not milked for the first three weeks after foaling, then they begin being milked twice a day, and this gradually is built up to six times a day.

The milk is widely used in the manufacture of *koumiss*, a refreshing beverage used as a therapeutic food. It is incubated with a special culture which produces a lactic and alcoholic fermentation.

Mare's milk, which is very different from cow's, is apparently the only milk suitable for making *koumiss* and, as it is in short supply, there are plans for expanding the industry of dairy horse farming.

# The Olympic equestrian sports

It was not until 1952 that women were first allowed to take part in the Olympics, competing in the dressage only. By 1964, however, women could take part in all three Olympic equestrian sports.

Equitation in the Olympic Games is represented by three different sports, eventing, show jumping and dressage.

The Fédération Equestre Internationale (FEI), the governing body for the equestrian sports at the Olympic Games, lays down strict rules and regulations, under which all the equestrian competitions are run.

In the modern Olympic Games, equestrian sport was included for the first time in 1912 at Stockholm. The programme for these first Olympic Equestrian Games consisted of individual dressage with a maximum of six riders per nation; a three-day event with teams of four riders of which three counted towards the team championships; show jumping which had two separate competitions, a team competition with four riders per nation of which three counted, and individual jumping in which six riders were allowed to compete. A team Dressage Championship was added in 1928, when the number of individuals was cut to three or four.

At the first Olympics in Stockholm, ten nations were represented but only Sweden and Germany sent full teams. Other countries such as Belgium, Britain, France and the United States entered the same four horses and riders in several, if not all of the four competitions. How very different it is today, when the standard has risen so much, and it would be unlikely that any horse would compete in more than one discipline.

Sweden dominated the Games, winning all but the show jumping individual gold medal. However the success of the equestrian events at Stockholm ensured their inclusion in future Olympic Games.

Over the years the standards of the various competitions rose, Germany setting very high standards at the almost-perfectly-run Games in Berlin in 1936. No Olympic Games were held during the Second World War, so it was not until 1948 that they were held once more in Britain. They were easier than they had been in Berlin, and were the spark that started Britain on the road to success.

It was in 1952, in Helsinki, that non-commissioned officers and women were first allowed to ride, although women were permitted to compete in the dressage only. At the next Olympic Games staged in Stockholm in 1956 women were also allowed to compete in the show jumping. It was not until 1964 at the Tokyo Olympic Games that they gained parity with the men and were also allowed to ride in the three-day event.

Rider negotiating a lake on the cross-country phase of an event. He has his weight a little too far back and the horse looks rather unhappy but is going well nevertheless.

# Eventing

'Eventing', as it is commonly referred to, is a rather vague way of describing one of the fastest-growing and most exciting sports in the equestrian sphere.

The three-day event, as its name implies, is held over three days. The riders and horses compete in a dressage test on the first day, a speed and endurance test across country on the second day and showjumping on the third day. The concept of the three-day event came from an endurance test devised for military horses, and in some countries is still referred to as the 'military'. Originally it was an endurance test at working pace, with a section across country negotiating natural obstacles, and generally some form of steeplechase course was ridden at speed.

Equestrian events were included in the Olympic Games at Stockholm in 1912 largely at the instigation of Count von Rosen,

Master of the Horse to the King of Sweden. He realized their value in stimulating interest and improving standards of equitation both inside and outside military circles. Although in the early days competitors all came from the services, civilians gradually began to compete, until by the end of the Second World War the majority of competitors were civilians.

At the Paris Olympic Games in 1920, the three-day event first took place in its present form; that is, with dressage on the first day, endurance ride in two phases with the steeplechase in-between, followed by a cross-country ride on the second day, then show jumping on the third day.

Although the Olympic Games seek to test the skill and fitness of both horse and rider to the highest degree, most countries now have many one-day events, where competitors can train their horses, (and themselves) and so progress to the more demanding sport covering three days.

One-day events are also included in both riding club and Pony Club activities, clubs competing on a regional basis against one another, the winners going to the National Championships.

## Show jumping

We know that man has been riding the horse for around 4,000 years, but it is comparatively recently that he has used him to jump obstacles. Hunting has been a sport for centuries, but in the early days the British countryside was forested or had open plains; it was not until the Enclosures Act of the eighteenth century that farmers divided the land into the fields that are so familiar today. This was the legislation that made it necessary for hunting people to jump the walls and hedges that grew up as a result.

Competitive jumping is an even more recent innovation. The first records reveal that at the Royal Dublin Society's annual show in 1865 there were competitions for 'wide' and 'high' leaps. A year later there was a jumping competition in Paris, but this more resembled a cross-country competition. After a preliminary parade indoors, the competitors were sent into the country to jump over mostly natural obstacles. Russia too had jumping contests around this time; few records remain, most were destroyed in the Revolution.

In Britain, jumping became a part of the agricultural shows, and was first officially recorded at a show at the Agricultural Hall, Islington, North London, in 1876. Horses entered in the show classes were also eligible for the 'leaping', which was judged on style.

In 1883 the first National Horse Show was held at Madison Square Garden, New York; it is still one of the most important international shows.

In Europe, jumping quickly became widespread and by the turn of the century was quite well established. Although the Olympic Games at Stockholm in 1912 are regarded as the first Games to hold equestrian competitions, jumping was included in the Games in Paris in 1900. The following year, officers of the German, Italian and

46

possibly Swiss armies, participated in the first officially recorded International Show Jumping.

The first International Horse Show, later to become the Royal International Horse Show, was held in London in 1907. The organizing committee was truly international, the prize money was quite considerable, and the jumping was dominated by the Belgians and the Dutch.

By the Olympic Games at Stockholm in 1912, international show jumping was well established, although those early pioneers would have been unlikely to forecast the spectacular growth there has been in the sport since then. Judging used to be most complicated, ten

Show jumping is a very popular spectator sport. The innovation of electronic timing has proved not only an aid to judges, who no longer have to rely on pressing a stop-watch by hand, but also makes the sport more exciting for the spectator, who can watch each competitor's time against the clock.

Show jumping is a very professional and rewarding sport. Many of the competitions offer not only trophies to the winners, but large amounts of prize money from sponsors too. Here, Lucinda Prior-Palmer and Killaire receive the coveted Whitbread Trophy, at Badminton 1979.

points being given for each fence, then deductions made for faults. At some shows there was a judge for each fence, which must have led to considerable delays in producing a result.

It soon became imperative that there was a standardization of rules, for although the Fédération Equestre International, founded in 1921, governed international rules, they did not cover national competitions. As a result, national organizations were formed to lay down the rules under which show jumping contests were to be held.

In Britain it was not until after the Second World War that show jumping really got on its feet. This was mainly due to the inspiration of that great and dedicated man, Colonel Sir Michael Ansell who, whilst in a German prisoner-of-war camp, dreamed up many plans for the future. He was appointed chairman of the British Show Jumping Association at the end of 1944, and did much to improve the rules and standards of show jumping. It was during his time in office that the use of lathes, thin pieces of wood laid along the tops of fences, were abolished. Their use caused many disputed results, lathes easily being dislodged by the wind or a horse's tail, and led to the abuse of horses, when riders endeavoured to teach them to jump 'clean'.

The introduction of a timed jump-off brought many changes, but most apparent was that it favoured a better class of horse, the very heavy hunters being at a disadvantage. With better horses competing, combinations and related distances were introduced.

A show jumper's basic training should be much the same as for other horses, as described in the section on dressage. A young horse should be quietly broken and trained to go forward freely on the bit during his first year. He should then be *taught* to jump, not just made to negotiate obstacles as best he can. He should be lunged over trotting poles, then gradually a small jump should be introduced at the end of the poles. This can be made a little larger, until he is quite able to cope with jumping a fence of about 27 in (70 cm) from a trot on the lunge. Only after this work on the lunge has become established should a horse be asked to cope with the added burden of a rider on his back when jumping.

Show jumping has become a very professional sport, although very few international riders are prepared to call themselves professional, thereby excluding themselves from the Olympic Games. Whereas there is little money to be made from eventing, this is not the case with show jumping. An event horse will probably not compete at more than a dozen horse trials in a year, but a show-jumper will compete in that number of competitions in a week, and will do so for several months at a time. With sponsors putting up large amounts of prize money, a top-class show-jumper is capable of earning several thousand pounds in a year. Consequently top-class jumpers demand very large amounts of money, some horses being sold for £75,000 or more.

The sport is not only big business as far as the sale of horses, but it has also become one of the most popular forms of public entertainment. Wide television coverage has brought it into the homes of millions and made it a popular spectator sport.

Famous show jumping personalities like the d'Inzeo brothers,

Harvey Smith, David Broome and Eddie Macken have become household names. Many riders have one good horse which takes them to the top, the media proclaim them as stars, but when that horse comes to the end of its career they are heard of no more. To stay at the top, one needs to have a constant supply of up-and-coming horses, and a dedication to the sport that keeps one there for year after year, through bad times as well as good ones.

## Dressage

The word dressage is a French word, derived from the verb *dresser*, meaning 'to train'. This name was not applied to riding until the eighteenth century, whereas the training of horses in a classical from can be traced to the fourth or fifth century BC. The Greeks studied the training of horses as an artistic and pleasurable accomplishment as well as improving the performance of their cavalry. One of the earliest horse masters was a cavalry general called Xenophon, who laid down the principles in a book, some of which still exists and is valid today. The Greeks also discovered that a quiet and sympathetic approach in training these powerful animals led to the best results. Over the centuries, dressage has developed to different degrees in different countries. It has always flourished in the more advanced civilizations; an activity requiring such patience and applied intelligence has never had a place in poor or primitive societies.

Dressage, as we know it today, has developed from the need to have easily controlled horses. Troopers unable to control their horses with one hand during battle were of little use. Many of the high-school (*haute école*) movements performed by the Spanish Riding School are movements used in battle hundreds of years ago.

During the Renaissance, dressage began to develop much along the lines we know today. It was performed by the military as part of their training; also by wealthy individuals who regarded it as part of a complete education, performing at royal courts and similar centres of culture. By the beginning of the twentieth century most of the courts had disappeared, which left the military as the main source of dressage accomplishment. The Second World War brought an end to the military establishments, which meant that it was up to civilians to take the lead.

Dressage was included in the first equestrian Olympic Games at Stockholm in 1912. Military riders dominated the Games until the outbreak of the Second World War. At first only individuals competed, but at Amsterdam in 1928, a team dressage competition was held for the first time. The Olympic Games in Helsinki in 1952 saw some more memorable changes, when non-commissioned officers and women were allowed to ride for the first time; since when women have won individual dressage medals at every Olympic Games.

The training of the horse may be broken down into three phases. The first breaking-in, produces a physically fit horse, going forward freely and calmly in a natural attitude, on the bit at the three basic paces. This should be obtained in the first year of training.

49

The Riding Hall of the Spanish Riding School, in the Hofburg, Vienna. This horse is performing the *levade*, a movement first used in battle, by which the enemy could be stabbed at from above. Like all the 'airs above the ground', it is performed without stirrups.

The second phase produces a gradual engaging of the hindlegs through growing flexibility of the quarters, the neck and head will be raised as the hindquarters propel the body forward. A head carriage should gradually be obtained at the rider's demand, by flexion at the poll. The maximum length of a horse's stride will be developed by suppling exercises, such as circles, serpentines, half-halts, change of pace and transitions from one pace to another. The horse's balance will also be improved by doing work on two tracks, shoulder-in, half-pass and *demi-pirouettes*. Additionally, work outside the school, over fences and across varying terrain should also be part of the basic training of all horses for whatever field of equitation they are destined.

The third phase, most frequently referred to as 'dressage' is the more advanced training where a horse specializes. If the goal is *haute école* the horse gradually progresses to near perfection of suppleness and obedience, where an image is created of the horse moving lightly and freely on its own. The forces of the horse must harmonize to allow perfect balance in motion; where constant eagerness to advance never disrupts calmness, or disturbs straightness of movement. Instant response to the rider's slightest aids, whatever is demanded, all go to build the picture of harmony.

Dressage has been performed in Vienna by the Spanish Riding School for several centuries. No definite date can be given to the foundation of this establishment, but it is known that an outdoor school was laid out in 1565. What is certain is that it is the oldest riding academy in the world where classical equestrian art has been practised in its purest form to the present day.

50

# Riding for sport and leisure

## Hunting

Hunting has long been a sport in Britain, probably since the Norman Conquest; however the fox did not become established as the main quarry until the middle of the eighteenth century. By the middle of the nineteenth century, due to the industrial revolution, more people could afford to hunt, and subscription hunts came into being. They hunted smaller areas than had the great 'hunting dukes', but were much more organized. All was not well during the period of change, when the titled gentry probably owned the hounds and were the landlords of most of the country over which hounds hunted, but the subscribers paid the hunting bills. Many disagreements arose between landlords and followers, some of which took years to settle; some of them still have not been fully resolved today.

We look back on those days, when there were no wire fences, or motorways or artificial fertilizers and regard them as the heyday of hunting. In fact there was much room for improvement; with none of the problems that our industrial age has brought, hounds used to be pushed along very fast. Wealthy people had little regard for their horses, who, unclipped, and probably not too well fed or fit, were frequently ridden to dropping point, many of them dying of exhaustion at the end of the day. The huge fields that followed hounds had little consideration for the farmers, for their crops or land. Foxes were not plentiful in some areas, and bagged foxes were quite commonplace.

The First World War changed all this, people began to realize that the farmer must be respected, and they began to appreciate hunting for what it should be; and not treat it just as a race across country. Proficient and dedicated grooms looked after hunters to the very best of their ability, they took pride in getting them properly fit and keeping them sound. The Second World War could well have been the end of hunting, but due to a few dedicated and tireless enthusiasts it has survived. Today it is more widespread than ever before, and a much wider cross-section of the public enjoy the thrills of riding to hounds.

We must define hunting as the pursuit of a wild animal in its own environment by man, with the aid of a pack of hounds. Drag hunting is the exception, as then a trail is artificially laid by man for hounds to follow.

51

The fox is the most frequently hunted quarry, but some packs hunt other animals. Jackals are hunted in South Africa and southern India; kangaroo, wallaby and deer in Tasmania. Hares are hunted by harriers, beagles and basset hounds in Britain, Ireland and New Zealand. The USA and Canada have numerous packs of foxhounds, some harriers and several drag hunts.

In Europe foxhunting has become very limited due to the spread of rabies, chiefly carried by foxes. No hunting of wild animals is allowed in Germany, but there are several drag hunts in existence. There is limited foxhunting in both Italy and Portugal.

Hunting is found principally in Britain, which boasts about 200 hunts; Ireland having some thirty packs. All forms of hunting, especially foxhunting have become enormously popular since the end of the Second World War, many hunts relying on the farmers in the country, who are hunting enthusiasts themselves, for much of their support. It has also become increasingly expensive, not only the subscriptions, but the cost of keeping a horse, and equipping both it and the rider in correct hunting attire. Many of the fashionable packs have too many supporters, and have increased their subscriptions drastically in an effort to reduce the size of their 'fields', so that only those of considerable means can still afford to hunt. There are many smaller packs, with rough or hilly countries, that still have very modest subscriptions and are only too pleased to welcome any supporters they can get.

The introduction of hunt supporters' clubs has meant that many more people are involved with the hunts. An enormous number of people, who for one reason or another, cannot be mounted to follow the hunt, do so in cars, on motor-cycles, bicycles or even on their feet. These people, by belonging to the local hunt supporters' club, take an interest in the hunt and feel involved.

## Drag hunting

Drag hunting has been introduced to England in the southern counties, where it is becoming an increasingly popular sport. Drag hunting also takes place in Europe, particularly in Germany, where the hunting of animals is illegal.

An artificial trail of scent is 'laid', usually by someone on horseback dragging an old sack soaked with a strong-smellng solution on a piece of rope. The pack of hounds is then taken to the area where the trail begins, and they pick up the scent.

The pack of hounds then hunts the artificial trail, with the mounted followers following as in a normal hunt. The object is to give riders the chance to negotiate natural country as they do when foxhunting, but as the line can be pre-determined it is arranged with the farmers in the locality so that young grass and other growing crops can be avoided.

The time may well come in the future when drag hunts will increase in number and take over from foxhunting. This will undoubtedly change things a lot in the country, where many country-born people have a great knowledge about the ways of the fox in particular, and also of the hare and deer in those regions

*Opposite*: Leicestershire in England has provided good foxhunting for over two hundred years – this is the Cottesmore Hunt, near Oakham. Silk hats, a scarlet coat and a lady riding side-saddle, elegant in a veil and dark habit, complete a picturesque traditional scene.

where they are hunted. It is this interest that has helped to preserve these animals, and to prevent them being exterminated because of the damage they cause.

However, with the ever-increasing cost of land, there are more farmers who are not happy to have several hundred mounted followers galloping over their land, particularly in wet weather. If it can be arranged for the trails to be laid where followers will cause the minimum damage to the farmer, then doubtless drag hunting will increase in popularity over the next few decades.

## Polo

Probably the oldest of all mounted sports, polo is known to have been played about 600 BC. Matches between Persians and Turkomans are described in ancient Persian manuscripts. Although there were more players on each side, the size of the pitch remains the same today.

The game spread to China, Japan, India and Asia Minor. British soldiers in India soon latched on to the sport, the Silchar Club, the oldest polo club in the world, being formed in 1859. The rules laid down by this club form the basis of the rules today.

In 1869 the game was introduced into Britain; the first recorded match in 1871 took place between the 9th Lancers and 10th Hussars. Shortly after this the first British rules were drawn up by the Hurlingham Polo Association.

Polo soon spread across the Atlantic, into the USA and South America, where it has become a major international sport. The first international match took place in 1886 with a series of matches between Britain and America for the Westchester Cup.

In Argentina, polo became an instant success; it became the biggest breeder of polo ponies, and a flourishing trade exporting ponies, particularly to Britain, was established.

Polo is a game played by two teams of four players, mounted on horseback. The grass ground used is 300 yards (274 m) long by 160 yards (148 m) wide if boarded, or 200 yards (182 m) wide if not boarded. The goals are marked by goal posts at each end, 10ft (3 m) high and 24 ft (7.3 m) apart. The ball is 3 inches (7.6 cm) in diameter, weighing $4\frac{1}{4} - 4\frac{1}{2}$oz (120 – 127 g). Balls used to be made from the root of the willow tree, which in Tibet was known as *pulu*, from whence the game derives its name.

Each player carries a polo stick, which must be carried in the right hand. The stick is made of cane, varying in length from 48 – 54 ins (121 – 137 cm) according to the needs of the player and the size of his pony. It has a cylindrical head 8 – 9 ins (20 – 23 cm) long, the ball being hit with the centre of the long side of the head.

Both horse and rider need protective clothing, a helmet and knee pads for the rider, and boots or bandages for the pony. Ponies usually have their manes hogged and their tails plaited up to prevent them interfering with the swing of the stick.

In India, some ponies used were scarcely 12 hh, the height limit in 1876 being 13.2 hh, while in Britain it was 14.0 hh. Later it was increased to 14.2 hh, then after the First World War, it was

abolished. Today most ponies are around 15.1 hh, although some as large as 16 hh are used.

Polo is the fastest team game in the world; it is played mostly at the gallop, and speeds of up to 30 mph (48 kph) can be reached. Consequently the ponies need to be changed and rested; the game is therefore split into periods or 'chukkas' of seven and a half minutes each. When a foul occurs the timekeeper stops his clock immediately the umpire's whistle is blown, then restarts it when play resumes. Consequently a chukka may last for well over the seven and a half minutes, although that is the actual time that the game is in play. Each match lasts a little under one hour and six chukkas are played, although in Argentina they sometimes play eight. There are three-minute breaks between the chukkas, with five minutes for half-time. Every time a goal is scored the teams change ends.

The players need to be fit, strong and courageous, have a good eye for the ball and be mentally alert. Horsemanship is of less importance than in other equestrian sports, as the damaged mouths of many polo ponies will tell.

Polo in Windsor Great Park, near London. Protective leg bandages, hogged manes, bound-up tails and standing martingales are usually standard turnout. It is an exciting game to watch, fast and skilful.

## Hunter trials and cross-country team events

Hunter trials are still a sport for the genuine amateur rider, who has not the time, ability or a suitable mount to participate in the more demanding sport of horse trials.

Usually organized by hunts, over a course of natural fence, typical of the sort of country in which they are held, hunter trials normally take place either at the beginning or end of the hunting season. The rules under which these are run vary considerably and leave plenty of scope for improvement. Some will have a timed section in them, others are run with the fastest round being the winner. It would perhaps be impossible to lay down a set of rules that would suit all types of country and organization.

Most hunter trials run classes for horses of differing standards, the usual being a members' class for the local members of the hunt; a novice class where the horse and/or rider has not won more than a small amount of prize money, and an open class, where sometimes the prize money is quite generous.

One of the most recent concepts of equestrian sport is that of cross-country team events. The idea was first put into practice by Douglas Bunn at Hickstead during the 1970's, since when the sport has literally grown like wildfire. Although rules do vary from place to place, there is rather more continuity to them than with hunter trials.

Usually a team of four members has to negotiate a course of between one and a half to three miles (2.4 – 4.8 km) of mainly natural fences. The time of the first three members counts, the fastest team being the winners. In most cases the teams have to carry a certain weight; this may be a set weight for each rider, or a total weight for the team, which means that a lightweight rider does not have to unduly burden his horse with dead weight.

This is a sport which hundreds of people have competed in for the genuine fun of having a ride round a course. There is a danger though, with the large prize money offered by sponsors, that this one genuine amateur sport could become as professional as point-to-pointing has done; hopefully it will not.

## Endurance and long-distance riding

Endurance and long-distance riding are two aspects of equestrian sport which have recently become popular, where man and horse participate together. They are enjoyed by a very wide cross-section of the riding public, using a great variety of horses and ponies. Although certain types of horse have featured most frequently in the awards, most riders, on an average horse, with due care and proper preparation can get themselves and their mount fit enough to compete in and enjoy these sports.

The USA is generally regarded as the birthplace of the sport. In 1919 the US Cavalry set up tests to compare the qualities of Arabian and Thoroughbred horses for use as remounts. Horses and riders had to cover 300 miles (483 km), split into 60 miles (96 km) per day

*Opposite*: Roland Fernyhough and Judy Crago's Bouncer negotiate the alarming-looking Derby Bank at Hickstead, going straight down it; this is the safe way to tackle this obstacle, which is part of the show jumping course.

57

for five days. Much was learnt about the care, conditioning, feeding and treatment of horses during these tests, and the annual Vermont One-hundred-mile Three-day Competitive Trail Ride (160 km) was started to make use of the knowledge thus gained.

Since then numerous other endurance rides have been instigated, varying in length from 20 miles to 100 miles (32 – 160 km). One of the toughest is the Western States Trail Ride, often known as the Tevis Cup Ride. Riders cover 100 miles in a day following the trail of the old Pony Express route. Competitors set out from Tahoe City, Nevada, and follow the hazardous trail over the Sierra Nevada Mountains that the Wells Fargo Express riders used. On the route they climb 9,500 feet (2,900 m) passing through snow and the cold winds of the Squaw Pass; then on through 100°F (38°C) heat, in El Dorado Canyon on route to Auburn, California.

During the ride there are three one-hour stops when the horses are checked by veterinary surgeons immediately they arrive. Each horse is checked again thirty minutes later and unless the pulse rate has returned to seventy beats per minute or less, the horses are not allowed to continue.

About 40 per cent of the 175 riders allowed in the Tevis Ride are eliminated each year. All competitors who complete the route within the twenty-four-hour time limit are given one of the famous silver and gold belt buckles. The winner is the fastest fit horse to

Veterinary examination before the Tom Quilty Endurance Ride, Australia. It is ridden over an up-hill-down-dale bushland course.

complete the distance, and times of less than twelve hours are quite commonplace. Prizes are also awarded for the horse in best condition after the ride.

So popular is this sport in the United States that there are now over thirty 50 and 100 mile (80 and 160 km) endurance rides, with between fifty and 200 competitors in each.

Long distance trail rides also require a fair measure of endurance, but they take place at a much slower pace and without the competitive element. Groups of riders, usually riding Western style, ride through scenic country for several days, camping out at night to appreciate the companionship of their fellow riders and their mounts.

In Australia endurance riding was a necessity, first for the explorers, and then the pioneers. As a sport it has seen a rapid growth since the Quilty Cup was first contested in 1966. Tom Quilty donated a valuable gold cup as a prize to stimulate interest and encourage good horsemanship in Australia. Run for 100 miles (160 km) over a tough course in the Blue Mountains of New South Wales where temperatures and humidity soar, this race was first won by Gabriel Stecher on a pure-bred Arab stallion which he rode bareback in just under eleven-and-a-half hours. Since then times have been reduced to a little over ten hours. Buckles are awarded for finishing in twenty-four hours.

A national association has been formed to guide the sport along the right lines. Numerous endurance rides are now included in the calendar, the Sydney Veterinary School giving much assistance with the essential veterinary work required.

Endurance riding also thrives in New Zealand; the National Association, although young, is guiding the rapidly growing sport along the right lines. The rules are based on the rules for the Tevis and Quilty rides. At present the longest ride is 75 miles (120 km) but it is hoped to run a 100 mile (160 km) ride soon. Rides are normally run over varied terrain and include some steep climbs; sudden changes in the weather can cause further hazards by making some of the going very boggy.

South Africa, another country that has an enthusiastic association, runs its National Championships over three days, covering 130 miles (208 km). The ride is run over varied terrain and judged as an endurance ride, the rules being taken from the Tevis Ride, even though it covers three days.

Long distance riding got under way in Britain in 1965 when the first Golden Horseshoe Long Distance Ride was held over 50 miles (80 km) of Exmoor country. Initially little was known about this sport; most competitors based their plans on the experience of people riding in the Tevis Cup. The ride was undoubtedly a great success, and the following year saw many enthusiastic riders entering. Inevitably there were problems, with excessive demands being made on unfit and unsuitable horses by inexperienced riders.

As a result the British Horse Society became involved, and they, together with the Arab Horse Society, have drawn up strict rules governing the running of competitions. Qualifying rounds now operate, where horse and rider have to cover a course of approximately 45 miles (72 km). The finals are held over two days,

Fording the River Barle on the 75 mile (120 km) Golden Horseshoe ride, on Exmoor, south-west England.

50 miles (80 km) being covered the first day, and subject to satisfactory veterinary tests a further 25 miles (40 km) are undertaken on the second day.

In 1973 the Endurance Horse and Pony Society was formed, which is concerned with the management of rides, and the information gained from veterinary research during the rides. The first 100 mile (160 km) ride was held in the New Forest in 1975, the winning time being twelve hours 1 minute. A points system is in operation, with trophies for horses gaining the highest points during the year.

In Germany most rides fall into the endurance category, and are between 50 and 100 miles (80–160 km) in length. With no hunting, endurance riding offers an alternative sport from the more usual indoor riding sports. At present the rules are rather different from other countries, the fastest horse over the course being the winner, and condition only being taken into consideration in the event of a tie. Also bonus and penalty points are awarded at various stages.

It is hoped that an endurance riding association will soon be started in Denmark, where there is also much interest in the sport. Other countries are bound to follow soon in this rapidly growing sport.

Over the years a type of horse has emerged as the most suitable. In nearly every instance it has been the Arab or part-bred Arab that has come out on top. The heavy hunter, or family cob has very rarely figured in the awards, the light, athletic type of horse having the advantage. Many breeders of Arabs now prove their stock by competing in long distance and endurance rides. Any defects come to light, so that it is to be hoped that these rides may well improve the breed by only the fittest and soundest animals being used for breeding purposes.

## Hacking and leisure

Many thousands of people ride just for the joy of sitting on a horse and seeing the countryside from this different aspect. There are many horses and ponies kept by people who will never hunt or take part in any competitive sport, but who simply ride for the pleasure they derive from it. There are also many hundreds of stables scattered throughout the length and breadth of Britain who keep horses and ponies for hacking or trekking.

Most children begin their riding career by having lessons at a local riding school. These naturally vary from school to school; it is wise to do some homework before deciding on one, and to find a school that is approved by the British Horse Society. This will mean that the school comes up to the standards of teaching and horse care that the society lays down, and that most of the many pitfalls involved with riding can be avoided. Most schools will give lessons on the art of riding, so that in time the pupil will become experienced enough to be able to take a horse or pony out hacking in the countryside.

Many people decide on a trekking holiday in the summer. It is obviously an advantage to be able to ride before embarking on this type of holiday, but some centres do cater for complete beginners. The first few days will be devoted to teaching the pupil how to handle and ride his mount before any actual trekking takes place.

Some parts of Britain obviously lend themselves to trekking more than others. The areas round the New Forest, Exmoor and Dartmoor naturally spring to mind. Wales has many first-class centres throughout the country, so too do the Lake District and Scotland.

Again some homework is of great importance before deciding where to go. Firstly obtain a guide of approved centres, then study it to decide a centre that caters for the right category of riders. It will spoil a holiday completely to choose somewhere that goes on long all-day treks if the rider is not sufficiently experienced or fit to cope with many hours in the saddle.

Apart from trekking centres where ponies and horses are provided, there are several that cater for riders with their own horses. The prospect of a week or two in different surroundings, with good stabling and comfortable accommodation appeals to many riders. The costs need not be outrageous, and for those keen to improve their horsemanship, lessons are often available.

Riding abroad has added attractions; the prospect of galloping along sun-drenched beaches in foreign places appeals to many

Hacking through the beechwoods of Kent, south-east England, on a fine day in autumn. Riders need to be on the lookout for dogs and children.

people. Again the rider must beware; there are many pitfalls to be avoided. Again, the ill-fed, badly cared-for horse that plods its weary way over the same bit of sand day after day will add little sparkle for the holiday maker. Also not to be forgotten is the fact that many people enjoy the pleasures of the beach on their own two feet! and it is frequently impracticable or illegal to ride on the seashore.

So far the emphasis has been mainly on holidaying with horses. There are of course thousands of people who ride and just go hacking for the pleasure of hacking. There are those who live in beautiful areas who just like to appreciate the countryside from horseback. To take one's lunch on one's back, and just to ride quietly along country lanes and bridlepaths drinking in the country air, smells and sounds must be one of the most restful and rewarding forms of country sports. For the young, and the not-too-young the pleasures of hacking can be many – not for them the cut and thrust of the hunting field or the competitive element of so many equestrian sports, but the quiet pleasure of the countryside shared with a faithful companion on which to ride.

## Showing

For hundreds of years man has wished to prove his stock better than other people's; racing as we know took place several centuries BC, but the concept of showing horses originated about two hundred years ago. The modern horse show has developed considerably since the Second World War; the classes are now so many and varied that the larger shows need four days or more, with several rings in constant use, to get through the comprehensive schedule.

Judging horses has, and always will be a matter of personal opinion of the judge or judges. There are however guidelines to which all judges must endeavour to adhere.

The most important consideration is that the animal, of whatever type or breed, is suited for the purpose for which it is intended. The thought of giving a prize to a Thoroughbred in a class intended for cart-horses is absurd. The conformation of horses will always be a subject about which individual opinions vary, but generally speaking the design of the horse should be suited to the work it is required to do; for example, the American Standardbred, selectively bred with a long back to enable him to cover more ground when on the race track, would be ill-suited for pony trekking in mountainous country.

In ridden classes, both the ride and manners of the horse must have a strong bearing on the results. All show animals must also possess that hard-to-define quality of 'presence' which catches the eye of all who look on them, and says 'look at me, I'm the greatest'.

Still considered the most important of showing classes in Britain are the hunter classes, for the ideal hunter is also likely to make a top-class show jumper, event or dressage horse. The high prices these animals command will always keep the show ring a shop window for prospective buyers. Hunter classes fall into two main categories; ridden hunters, and those led in-hand.

The ridden hunter classes at larger shows are divided into different weight categories, with additional classes for small, novice, four-year-old and ladies' hunters. In Britain hunters are only expected to perform on the flat, although the classes for working hunters, where they are required to jump a small course of natural fences, are becoming increasingly popular.

In the USA all hunters are expected to show their paces over

fences as well as on the flat, favouring the genuine hunter as opposed to the good-looking horse who may be a useless performer across country.

There is a great art in showing horses, more particularly in the ridden classes. A good rider will be able to accentuate the best points of a horse and can often disguise some doubtful aspect of its conformation or action. Top professional riders are in great demand by owners of show horses, some of whom rarely see their horses from one appearance in the ring until the next.

The normal procedure for show classes is for the animals to file into the ring. They all show their paces at the walk, trot, canter and gallop, then the judges will call them into line in a provisional order. The horses are then ridden by either one or two judges, following

which they are 'stripped off', their saddles removed, and they are led out in-hand. The judges will inspect their limbs, or any aspect about which they may have doubts, then the horse will be walked and trotted in-hand so the judges can see their action and how straight they move. When they have been re-saddled and mounted, they walk around once more before being called in again in the final placings.

Led hunters are shown 'in-hand'; there are normally classes for one-, two- and three-year-olds as well as for brood mares and foals. These classes are basically supported by genuine enthusiasts, who breed a few young horses, mainly as a hobby. Although winning is all-important to a few, most use the opportunity of showing their animals as one of the best forms of education that a youngster can

A country horse show. A pairs driving class is in progress; the next event is to be show jumping. A van is arriving with a wall jump and the competitors are walking the course, in order to memorize the order of jumps and the distance between each.

65

A prize-winning Arab mare. The fine silky mane and tail hair is left natural and untrimmed with this breed.

have. Again the professional showman can make the led horse look or move that little bit better than an inexperienced leader; but with no saddle or riding expertise it is less easy to disguise any shortcomings. In-hand classes are judged on conformation and movement, the animals being inspected and run out in-hand after a preliminary walk around.

There has been a tendency amongst the serious showing fraternity to produce very large and mature-looking young horses. These look magnificent and usually take home the ribbons (rosettes), but there is a serious danger that by forcing their development too rapidly a number of problems will occur when they are expected to do some hard work later in their lives.

Other ridden classes at show that may be seen are the cob classes; a rapidly diminishing type of horse that is little in demand today. Hacks, once so popular when the gentry passed the time of day taking a ride in the great city parks, are gaining some popularity once more. The beauty and grace they must possess should be combined with a high degree of schooling.

Every country has its own special type of breed of horse that it favours. The Arab is shown fairly world-wide; fortunately it is now seen much more under saddle than used to be the case. In the USA the Tennessee Walking Horse is bred almost exclusively for the show ring, a spectacle that will be observed nowhere else in the world. Societies for coloured horses, such as the palomino and spotted horse, have their own special classes, as do nearly all native

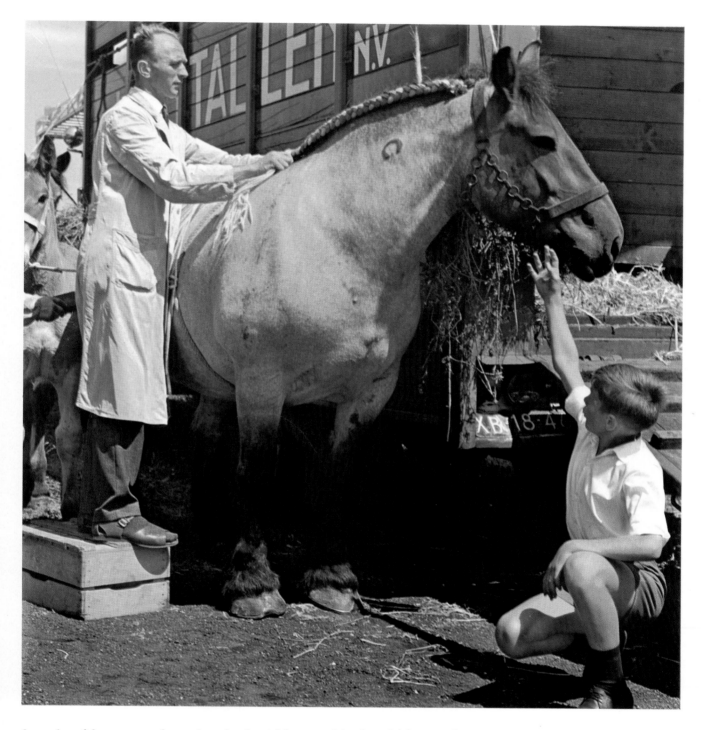

breeds of horses and ponies, both ridden and in-hand classes for breeding stock.

   The heavy horses must not be forgotten; not only do they have their own breed classes, but even their own breed shows. It is good to see competitions for these magnificent horses, so that the younger generations may appreciate the skill that was needed before the advent of the tractor.

A Dutch Draught Horse being prepared for a show, the mane plaited with coloured wool threads. The brand mark of an inverted horseshoe shows on the offside of the neck.

# Competition and
# pleasure driving

Horses were, in the first instance, used as pack-horses; then it was discovered that a larger burden could be transported if it was tied behind a horse and pulled along. Originally, a pole was attached to either side of the horse by means of straps round the horse's neck and girth; the ends of the poles were left to drag on the ground and the load was tied across them.

The Ancient Britons used these first rudimentary sledges; no doubt on the unmade forest tracks, they worked better than wheels. Queen Boudicca used chariots with two wheels and a pole, drawn by two, three, or four horses abreast. These vehicles were used for fighting and racing but it is unlikely they were used for transporting passengers or luggage.

During the Roman occupation, the magnificent roads that we still use today were built; this would have made it easy for using horse-drawn vehicles. However after the Romans departed, the roads fell into disrepair and the task of hauling a wheeled vehicle through the deep winter mud must have been impracticable. It was therefore easier to ride on horseback than to travel in a wheeled vehicle. Carts were used on farms about a thousand years ago, but these agricultural vehicles were not suitable for passenger transport.

The horse litter was a method of transport devised to transport passengers who were unable to ride. A box-like device was attached to poles fore and aft, which were harnessed to two horses. This avoided the use of wheels and was a method, albeit a rather precarious one, of transporting aged or sick people. Litters were also used for state occasions, when they were lavishly decorated with rich trappings, as also were the horses. Catherine of Aragon, first wife of Henry VIII, rode in a litter in 1509; this was presumably considered a superior form of conveyance to a covered chariot, which without springs must have been an uncomfortable mode of transport.

Over the next fifty years there must have been an improvement in the building of vehicles, because in 1553 Queen Mary Tudor rode to her coronation in a four-wheeled chariot drawn by six horses. Shortly after this, the first private coaches were built, and during the next fifty years they were in general use among the gentry, although only in the larger towns and cities where the road surfaces were suitable.

The stage or flying-wagon was also developed during the latter half of the sixteenth century. These were heavy, cumbersome

vehicles, used for carrying passengers and goods from the larger country towns to London. Hauled by a team of six, eight or ten heavy horses, they were driven by a wagoner either on foot or mounted, and probably only averaged about three miles (4.8 km) an hour. This form of transport was given the name flying-wagon because it was considered such an improvement on the previous form of transport, the pack-horse!

The beginning of the seventeenth century saw the introduction of what we know today as the taxi-cab. This was a four-wheeled hackney coach, the word hackney coming from the French word *haquenée*, meaning a horse for hire. Usually these coaches were vehicles that had been in private service but had been replaced by more modern coaches. By 1634 a stand of hackney coaches was established in The Strand, but they proved so popular that they caused traffic jams in the narrow London streets. A year later King Charles I issued a royal decree forbidding their use in the City unless the passenger was making a journey over three miles (4.8 km). Sedan chairs were also invented at this time, and their use somewhat relieved the situation.

However over the next twenty-five years the number of hackney coaches increased so much that they had become a public nuisance.

The Lord Mayor's Show, London. The Lord Mayor's Coach is accompanied by two pikemen of the Company of Pikemen and Musketeers of the Honourable Artillery Company.

69

As a result they were forbidden to stand in the streets and had to remain in their yards until they were needed. Eventually a law was passed by King Charles II limiting hackney carriages to 400 licensed holders. This led to those unable to obtain a licence setting up in towns surrounding London and driving up each day.

Stage coaches were started about 1640, but they were heavy, virtually unsprung vehicles, and the roads were so bad that they could only be used in summer. They were also very slow, the journey from Exeter to London taking four days. In the 1660's a cumbersome type of coach pulled by a postillion-driven pair was used. 1663 saw the first turnpike gate on the Great North Road collecting tolls; this was a very unpopular move, but the revenue collected led eventually to much improved roads throughout England. This is turn brought about the improvement of coach building, and thus the demand for lighter, faster horses. As coaches became more sophisticated, more horses were harnessed together to pull them. With the roads still poor in some places, probably six horses would be needed to get a heavy coach through the mud; but in London the gentry used as many as eight horses just for show, as a form of one-upmanship.

The Great Fire of London in 1666, when much of the town was destroyed, had its compensations. When rebuilding took place, the streets were widened and much improved, thereby making the passage of traffic much easier and resulting in the number of hackney coaches being increased. Much improvement to the roads, financed by the turnpike tolls, had resulted by the early eighteenth century. A stage coach ran between London and York three days each week, taking only four days for the 200 mile (322 km) journey. Although much of the road was good, there were still bad sections where it was quite usual to get stuck, resulting in long delays while extra horses were brought to help the coach team move the vehicle. The design of coaches had also improved, but they tended to be top-heavy when loaded and were very inclined to overturn. The traveller also had to contend with the possibility of 'hold-ups' by highwaymen, the heavy slow-moving coaches being easy prey for the often well-mounted outlaws.

There was room for eight passengers inside the coach, the remainder travelling outside, to begin with in a large open-topped basket over the rear axle; then later, when a lid was put on the basket, they travelled on the top of the coach. In cold weather passengers wrapped straw around their legs to try and keep warm. In the latter half of the eighteenth century, springs for coaches were invented; this was a great improvement, and a number of different kinds were tried to help relieve the discomfort to passengers and horses alike. The coaches ran more easily when sprung and this led to them being frequently overloaded. One tale describes a coach carrying thirty-four passengers plus baggage. By the end of the century, there was such an increase in the number of coaches and accidents that it became necessary to limit the height of the vehicles and the number of passengers.

For years the mail had been carried on horseback, but in 1784 the first mail coach was introduced and fifteen years later there were eight mail coaches leaving London each day. This brought about the creation of a new position, that of the mail guard, who travelled on the coach. He was responsible for the safe delivery of the mail and passengers and the punctual running of the coach. Mail guards had to have a thorough knowledge of the coaching service, be able to repair coach or harness, and in the event of becoming stuck, be able to ride one of the horses to deliver mail. He sat over the boot of the coach at the back, with a blunderbuss at the ready to ward off robbers.

The 'Golden Age of Coaching' lasted only from 1815 to about 1840, when the growth and reliability of the railway system brought about the decline of coaching. Improved roads during this time produced faster coaches, though none were considered finer that the Royal Mail, which were so punctual that the villagers used to set their timepieces by the coach passing through. As the Royal Mail was exempt from tolls, the turnpike gates were opened ready for them, the gatekeeper being warned of the approaching coach by the call on the coaching horn. Horses were changed at inns about every ten miles (16 km), this operation being perfected to a fine art and accomplished in a matter of seconds.

Coaching developed its own language; many of the terms are still used today although they are now applied to cars. Not all horses were of the highest standard, or in the best condition, some sick horses being used at night-time when they were less likely to be noticed. Horses were quite often used for two sessions each day, one stage in each direction. The average working life of a coach-horse on a fast run would only be about four years.

The many road or stage coaches, as opposed to mail coaches, were run by inn-keepers, under the same system as the mail coaches; but they were much slower as they only travelled by day. They also had to stop to pay the tolls at the many toll-gates on the route. The coaches were of a similar size, seating four people inside, but having seats for twelve on the top, unlike the limit imposed by the Post Office of only four passengers on the top of the mail coaches. The inside seats were more expensive, but the outside seats were more popular with the young men of the day, many of them keen to sit on the box-seat next to the driver and take a turn at the reins.

Driving a four-in-hand was a fashionable sport and the wealthy usually owned their own coaches. Many private coaches were built to the special requirements and whims of individuals all over the country. Several driving clubs were formed, the first of which stipulated that only barouche-landaus should be used, but as many young men had driven mail and stage coaches, this type of vehicle was eventually accepted and became known as a 'private drag'. These private drags were usually painted in their owner's colours with the crest painted on the doors and hind-boot. They could hold quite a number of friends on the top, and became very popular for use as grandstands from which to watch sport. A rear seat was built to take two liveried grooms, who would leap on to the coach as it moved off, after attending to the horses whilst the passengers climbed aboard.

In 1829 a three-horse public omnibus was introduced, the forerunner of our bus system. It carried twenty-two passengers and

Four-in-hand driven to a road coach on the marathon phase of a combined driving event. Vehicles are driven for several miles (kilometres) across country and along roads, at varying speeds to suit the terrain.

provided a library for interest during travel. The fast growing railway system severely curtailed the activities of the road coaches, but they were still used as links with the railways and to remote parts of the country where railways had not reached. Although the road and mail coaches lost their importance, horse transport was very much part of the British scene. Towards the end of the nineteenth century it was estimated that there were 30,000 horses working in and around London in different capacities, varying from fire fighting, general haulage such as delivering coal, to pleasure driving and funeral work.

With the invention and increased use of the internal combustion engine, coaching and horse transport in general suffered a severe decline. Enthusiasts still drove their horses for pleasure, but the 'Golden Age of Coaching' was past. Many vehicles were broken up and used for scrap; harness rotted and was thrown away. The petrol shortage during the Second World War caused a slight revival, when vehicles were uncovered and brought back into use.

The British Driving Society was founded in 1957, headed by that great enthusiast, Sanders Watney. Their first meeting was held at Royal Windsor Horse Show in 1958, when about forty turnouts were present. Since then their numbers have fluctuated somewhat, but at present driving is more popular than ever and better supported in all its forms that it has been for many years.

There are many different types of horses and ponies suitable for driving; there are however several ancient breeds that have been specifically bred to use in harness. Among these are the Hackneys, the high-couraged high-stepping horses now usually seen only in the show ring. Other heavier types of horse that have been used for driving for generations are the Cleveland Bays from Yorkshire, seen on many state occasions pulling the royal coaches; the Gelderland from Holland; the Holsteiner and Oldenburg from Germany, and the Kladruber from Austria. Many of the British native ponies prove excellent in harness and can be regularly seen in the ribbons throughout the country at most shows with driving classes. In the USA the Standardbred has been developed for harness racing, while France, Germany and Russia all have their own breeds of trotters.

## The Hackney (Britain)

The modern Hackney is a harness-horse with an extravagant high-stepping trotting action. They are descended from the Norfolk Roadster, a powerfully built animal that was bred as a utility horse and used by farmers for riding as well as driving. The advent of railways reduced the demand for riding horses, but carriage horses were still much sought after.

Hackneys go far back into British history, the trotting horse being mentioned in the early fourteenth century. The Hackney Horse Society was formed in 1883 when the breed was attracting attention from breeders far removed from the East of England. Hackneys have much Arab blood, almost all being descended from the Darley Arabian through his son 'Flying Childers'.

By the beginning of this century, Hackneys had established themselves in Britain and abroad as the finest harness horses in the world. The introduction of the motor car caused a great decline in the breed, only the best horses being retained. This resulted in a steady improvement between the two World Wars in the quality of Hackney horses, so that today the standard of animals is of the highest, with the result they are still much in demand abroad.

There are both Hackney horses and ponies, the characteristics of which are similar. They should have a small convex head, small muzzle and ears but large eyes. The high and crested neck should be longish and thick set, the shoulders flat and laid well back to allow free action of the forelegs. The withers are low, the body compact without great depth of chest, the tail set and carried high. The limbs should have flat bone, short cannon bone and long sloping pasterns, the feet round, fairly upright with good horn. The coat is fine and silky, the most usual colours being dark brown, black, bay and chestnut, frequently with much white on the legs. Height varies greatly, some standing up to 16.2 hh, whilst some ponies are only 12 hands; about 15 hands would be a usual size for a horse.

*Overleaf*: Concern showing on the faces of Yugoslavian competitors entering the watersplash 'hazard', Virginia Water. This is part of the marathon course of the Royal Windsor Horse Show's driving event, held in the Home Park in May.

Hackneys are very distinctive both whilst in motion and when resting. The shoulder action is free, with a high knee action, the leg being thrown well forward after a slight pause of the foot during each stride. The hindlegs have a similar if less pronounced action, with great flexion of the hock and stifle. A good Hackney must really cover the ground when he trots and have straight and true action with no dishing. At rest he should stand square, the front legs upright, the hindlegs well back covering as much ground as possible. The head is held high with an impression of alertness and of being on springs.

## The Cleveland Bay (Britain)

One of the oldest English breeds, the Cleveland Bay, originated in north-east Yorkshire and was used as a pack-horse in the seventeenth and eighteenth centuries. For the past two hundred years they have been used as general purpose horses, equally at home doing light farm work or taking the family to church or market.

They are usually bright bay in colour, though some darker bays are to be found. These versatile horses stand about 16 to 16.2 hh. The rather convex head tends to be on the large side and is carried on a long neck. The back also tends to be long but the loins and quarters are very strong. The limbs are short, clean and very hard with 9 in (22 cm) of bone. White, except for a very small star on the forehead, is not acceptable.

Cleveland bays are noted for their intelligence, sensible temperament, strength, stamina and longevity. They have the ability to pass on these characteristics to their progeny when crossed with other breeds. As a result of which they were much in demand abroad, especially during the nineteenth century, where they have influenced many horses throughout the world.

They have also made a name for themselves as carriage horses, proving particularly tough and reliable. Today they still are much in demand for driving and are kept, in addition to other places, at the Royal Mews and used on state occasions.

Cleveland Bays have also proved successful jumping horses, and when crossed with Thoroughbreds produce excellent heavyweight hunters and show-jumpers.

## The Oldenburg Horse (Germany)

Based on the Friesian horse, a very ancient breed from the Netherlands, the Oldenburg was developed in the region of that name as early as the seventeenth century. In Germany, during the eighteenth and nineteenth centuries several different breeds were introduced, including the Thoroughbred, Cleveland Bay and Hanoverian horses. This resulted in a coach-type horse that was very strong, and also noted for maturing early. After the First World War a heavier type of horse was preferred for use as a general farm horse; however by the end of the Second World War,

*Opposite*: A Hackney being exercised on a country road, showing the high knee action of the breed.

increased mechanization saw the decline of the heavier type, and a lighter sort of a horse, that could be used for riding, was developed.

The first Oldenburg horse breeding act was passed in Germany in 1819; it was amended in 1897 and again in 1923, entrusting the responsibility for the breed to the breed society. Oldenburgs are tall horses, standing 16.2 to 17.2 hh, but are surprisingly short-legged for their height. They have good bone, strong backs, and great depth of girth, with a kind nature, but yet they are bold. They make excellent harness horses and are in demand as such throughout the world; His Royal Highness Prince Philip has a team that he has regularly driven in competitions in this country and abroad.

## The Gelderland (Netherlands)

This excellent carriage horse was created as a breed in the last century when a mixture of imported stallions, most notably Norfolk Roadsters and Arabs, were used on the local mares in the Gelder province of the Netherlands. The best of the resulting offspring were bred together and gradually a type began to develop. Later East Friesian, Oldenburg and Hackney blood was added, but since the turn of the century only Anglo-Norman blood has been added.

Standing about 15.2 hh, the Gelderland is a strong active horse, usually chestnut in colour with white markings, although there are greys and even some skewbalds to be found. They have great presence and eye-catching action, making them excellent carriage horses; they are capable of doing light agricultural work, and are useful riding horses, the best proving themselves good show jumpers.

## The Standardbred (USA)

Harness racing was a popular feature of country fairs, particularly in the eastern states of the USA. In the early days several heats used to be held, and it was the winner of the most heats who took the honours. A tough horse with stamina was required and these were most frequently produced from crossing a Thoroughbred with the local harness horses. A Trotting Register was started in 1871; to qualify for registration a horse had to trot or pace a mile (1.6 km) in a standard time. For the trot this had to be less than 2.30 mins; hence the breed derived its name.

Standardbreds have many characteristics of the Thoroughbred, but tend to be a little heavier-boned, shorter in the neck and longer in the body. The head is not so refined as the Thoroughbred's; the ears tend to be longer and the nostrils capable of great dilation to cope with breathing in the extra oxygen required for racing.

## The Orlov Trotter (USSR)

Named after Count Alexius Grigorievich Orlov who founded the Khrenov Stud in Russia in 1778, the Orlov has become one of the most famous breeds of trotters.

The first trotter was a grey stallion named 'Bars First', descended from a white Arab stallion and out of a dun Dutch mare. He had valuable qualities that were later developed by the breeders.

Trotting races were held in Moscow at the end of the eighteenth century. As the sport developed during the nineteenth century, the Orlov horses were much in demand, and they became faster. They were also popular carriage horses. Until the development of the American Standardbred, the Orlovs were the best trotters in the world.

The Orlov has been used to improve many other breeds since it was first developed. They are a strong type of horse with a fairly heavy head, rather straight shoulders, long back with plenty of depth through the girth and strong legs with plenty of bone. Breeders have always preferred a tall horse, many of them standing up to 17 hh although 15.2 to 16.2 hh is more usual.

They are tough, long-lived horses, and although bred for harness are also used under saddle. The most usual colours are grey and black although there are bays and chestnuts.

# Horses at work

As far as horses are concerned, whatever man asks them to do, it is work; whether it be galloping down a racecourse, jumping over fences or pulling a plough. To the horse it makes little difference to distinguish between work and pleasure. However, for the purposes of this book we will define working horses as those who assist man with his work, as opposed to those ridden or driven for sport or pleasure.

When man first made use of the horse it was to help him with his daily life, mainly to assist with transport; first of all as a pack-animal

Trooping the Colour, part of the Queen's Birthday Parade Ceremony. HM The Queen, riding side-saddle, accompanied by HRH Prince Philip, takes the salute at Buckingham Palace, London. In spite of the pomp and splendour of the occasion, this is still just in a day's work for the horses.

Horses were used to help man transport things. Pack-horses were loaded with saddlebags and boxes.

Man soon realized that horses could transport much greater loads if pulled behind them, on sledges or carts, etc.

to carry loads, then to pull things behind him, to begin with on sledges and then with wheeled vehicles. Later man made more use of the horse, as a method of transport in war and then he was used extensively in agriculture.

As man has developed new forms of transport, namely the horseless carriage, which we know today as a car, so the role of the horse in transport has practically disappeared. There are some parts of the world, though, where horses are still used for transport, where there are no roads and a car or lorry are useless.

The magnificent carriages used by the wealthy a century ago, with matched teams of horses, are rarely seen outside the show ring, competitions or specially organized drives. Some heavy horses are still used in Britain and Europe for delivery purposes by breweries, who find it more economical to use horse-power for short journeys. Horses are also still used for agriculture (*see* Chapter 3).

Gone are the days when we summoned a hackney carriage to take us from one destination to another; today it is a taxi. Gone too are the days when tradesmen's deliveries were done with the help of a horse; there may still be a few milkmen who harness up their pony and cart, but they are very few and far between, in Britain at any rate.

Although thousands of horses are no longer used as they were even fifty years ago, horses are being used in new trades, mainly connected with the tourist industry. Pony trekking is growing not only in Britain but all over Europe and in the USA. Since the end of the Second World War there has also been a great upsurge of interest in the horse. Numerous riding schools have come into business to cope with this demand from a section of the public that previously had little contact with horses. With this great increase in riding schools, there have inevitably been cases where the welfare of the horses has been sadly neglected in preference to making financial gains. Several organizations, notably the British Horse Society, have gone to great expense and trouble to try to visit, advise, and approve where possible, thousands of riding schools. For those interested in learning to ride it is as well to only attend a riding school approved by one of the organizations concerned.

Another way in which the horse has helped man in recent years is by enabling thousands of disabled people to ride and thereby helping them to achieve independence. It has been proved beyond doubt that great medical benefit has been derived from disabled people riding. The personal triumphs witnessed by those who devotedly help on a voluntary basis each week are a worthy reward for the hours spent helping with the Riding for the Disabled.

There are many other fields where horses have assisted man with his work, a few of which we will look at in more detail.

## The Cavalry

The use of horses in warfare is one of the first roles they ever fulfilled. Horses made a soldier mobile when mounted and gave a commanding officer a much better view of how the battle was progressing, so he could assess the situation and command his troops accordingly.

During the Middle Ages, men with property were required to keep a horse ready for war. During the reign of Queen Elizabeth I the Spaniards were driving out non-Catholics in Europe with their superior cavalry. The Queen was so disgusted with her army when she reviewed it at the time of the Armada that she commanded her generals to breed chargers good enough to face those of Philip II.

During the seventeenth and eighteenth centuries, emphasis was placed on speed and manoeuvrability. The mounted musketeer or dragoon came into being; he usually fired from the halt or from the ground when dismounted; he was used to outflank enemy armies and produce a surprise element, whilst the infantry advanced head-on. During this period most countries had large state studs for providing their armies with horses. Also the great riding schools in Europe were established to train the cavalry officers in the art of equitation.

Charles II was so impressed by the French mounted royal bodyguard that he formed the first troop of Life Guards, the original Household Cavalry. Other regiments followed; the Royal Regiment

Soldiers of the Blues and Royals mounted squadron of the Household Cavalry on Horse Guards Parade, London, in winter. They are distinguishable from the Life Guards who wear white plumes in their helmets.

of Horse Guards, the Horse Grenadiers, Dragoon Guards and Light Dragoons.

At the end of the eighteenth century, with the development of field artillery, the Royal Horse Artillery, known as the 'Galloping Gunners', were formed to support the cavalry.

Large cavalry forces were used in all wars in Europe during the nineteenth century, but the improvement of guns and the development of the machine gun towards the end of the century had a dramatic effect on the cavalry. The losses to the regiments caused by machine guns, and the use of barbed wire, were devastating and the First World War resorted to trench warfare, with horses being used mainly for transport purposes of moving supplies.

Cavalry warfare came to an end in much the same area in which it began, in the steppes. In 1943 the German lines, under great pressure during the bitter winter, and unable to move their tanks, were attacked by Russian cavalry divisions, riding over the snow, firing machine carbines and throwing hand grenades. Then they disappeared over the horizon before the dazed Germans had time to collect themselves together to retaliate.

Since the end of the Second World War, the cavalry regiments of all armies have been reduced to the minimum. Not all the old glamour has gone; the horse still provides the cavalry officer with his sport, both in the hunting field, and in eventing, show jumping and polo. The mounted regiments of the Life Guards and the Blues and Royals fulfil many ceremonial duties, providing some of the best pageantry in London when they head many of the ceremonial parades including Trooping the Colour and other state occasions. The King's Troop of the Royal Horse Artillery are seen throughout the country at many shows where they perform exciting displays with their teams of horses and gun carriages. They also have an excellent mounted band and take their place in both royal and state ceremonies.

Several other countries still maintain cavalry regiments, but as in Britain these are used mainly to fulfil ceremonial duties at state occasions.

# The police

Police forces in many countries still retain mounted sections. Their duties include ceremonial escort, crowd control and public relations. A mounted policeman still commands a healthy respect from the majority of people, which his contemporary on foot can not. They are therefore at a great advantage when coping with large crowds of people, whether they are gathered for a festive occasion, or more commonly a street demonstration.

Even for traffic control he has the advantage that he is clearly visible, and has a better view than he would have if on foot. In Tokyo, where both traffic and pedestrians have reached saturation point, police horses are considered indispensable for controlling street crossings.

The London Metropolitan Police incorporated the first mounted

branch in 1839; today there are about 200 police horses in the London area, with mounted branches in Bath, Birmingham, Bristol and Manchester.

Among the world's most famous police forces are the Royal Canadian 'Mounties'. This is a semi-military force that was established in 1873 as the North-West Mounted Police. They covered some 300,000 square miles (776,997 sq km) of ungoverned territory and it was their duty to keep the peace between the 30,000 Indians who lived there and the increasing number of traders and settlers who encroached on the Indian homelands, threatening their large herds of buffalo. The climate and rugged terrain demanded a lot from these men and their horses in the way of courage and endurance. They were constantly in danger and needed to use all their ability both to survive and to keep the peace. They gradually brought law and order to the vast territories and the scarlet-coated 'mounties' became welcome figures.

In 1920 their duties were extended to cover the whole of Canada and they became known as the Royal Canadian Mounted Police.

Royal cavalry at the Palace, Katmandu, Nepal, waiting for HM King Birendra and HM The Queen to drive out of the gates for a ceremony. The cavalry is only used on special occasions. Their red helmet plumes are form the now-protected bird-of-paradise.

With mechanization the role of the 'Mounties' was diminished, but they still used horses on general duties until the Second World War. Today they still breed their own black horses, but they are restricted to fulfilling ceremonial duties, and for the famous musical ride. This spectacular display of horsemanship is performed throughout Canada and has been staged in many other countries both in America and Europe where it helps to promote good relations.

Whilst the stamp of horses used for the police forces throughout the world does vary – the Tehran Mounted Police ride fiery Persian stallions – the most important aspect is a calm temperament. In Britain a middleweight hunter type is usually chosen; the horses then undergo a very thorough training. They are carefully broken and given basic schooling up to quite a high standard. When this has been done then the specialized training is undertaken. They have to learn to ignore noises ranging from rowdy crowds of footballers with 'rattles', to brass bands and gunfire. They must also learn to stand and resist a pushing crowd, without any hint of kicking, also to walk over people lying down without treading on them, and up and down steps. Waving umbrellas, flags, fires and fire engines all have to be taken without becoming upset. When the horse is trained, it is most important to pair him up with a rider of the right temperament. Soon they become a team, and the rider is able to forget his horse and concentrate on the job at hand.

At the 'Horse of the Year Show' each autumn, there are special classes for police horses, when they are judged for their performance during a test including 'street nuisances' which are enacted by a group of volunteers.

## The circus

Horses have been used to entertain the public for several hundred years. Shakespeare referred to a horse called 'Morocco' in *Love's Labour's Lost* who 'danced' before crowded galleries in the courtyard of an Inn at Ludgate Hill, but it was not until the nineteenth century that the circus as we know it came into its own.

There are three main groups of horses used in the circus, the high school horse, the liberty horse and the vaulting or rosinback.

Thoroughbreds or Anglo-Arabs usually make the best high school horses; the Thoroughbreds are more impressive and show their action better than the smaller Arabs or Lipizzaners, but they are more difficult to train and so a compromise is often the best answer. It takes several years to bring a high school horse to perfection; the famous Schumann family were known world wide for outstanding performances on their beautiful grey stallions. Very careful and patient training are needed to bring the best out of high-school horses, who basically perform dressage type movements, with some rather more spectacular tricks added.

The liberty horses, usually bedecked with plumes attached to a glamorous harness, are very carefully matched for colour, size and type. Arab stallions are the most popular; they are small enough to fit a dozen into quite a small ring, and their good looks and great presence make them great eye-catchers. Training is begun

A member of the Royal Canadian Mounted Police. The prefix 'Royal' was bestowed on the force by Edward VII in recognition of its service. Their motto is 'Maintain the Right'.

86

individually on the lunge, the act gradually being put together after the horses have learnt to go forward, to stop and to change direction. The next step is to learn *pirouettes*, as these supple the horses and teach them to use themselves. The tone of the trainer's voice is more important than the words used, the horses must learn to be obedient, but must never be frightened. Frequently at the end of a liberty act, most of the horses leave the ring, and one or two perform individual acts such as walking on their hindlegs.

The third group of horses used in the circus are the rosinbacks; they must have wide level backs; be totally unperturbed and keep up a slow uninterrupted canter. They are usually a heavy type of horse that has little action behind the saddle and has ceased to be amazed by the antics of man. The bareback riding act is one of the most risky acts in the circus, not often appreciated by the audience who hold their breath in anticipation at the antics of the high-wire and flying trapeze artists. Frequently the rosinbacks are accompanied by a clown, who can draw a laugh from the audience by his feats of daring with the horses, such as swinging under their bellies, or hanging upside-down.

Circus horses on the whole tend to have quite a long life. After the initial training is complete they will probably have half an hour's practice in the morning, and then only ten minutes or so in the ring during the two acts each day. They are well-fed and well-groomed and many of them are still performing at the ripe old age of twenty or more.

# Famous people, places and horses

## People

### Lester Piggott

There are several famous names in the racing world; Fred Archer, Steve Donoghue and Gordon Richards all became legends in their lifetimes; but Lester Piggot is the only one to have achieved that status before he was twenty-five.

Born in 1935, Lester followed his father's footsteps into the world of racing. He has been riding since the age of three and had his first public ride, for his father, when he was only twelve. He first became Champion Jockey in 1960 at the age of only twenty-five, and has to date earned that coveted title no less than nine times.

Lester's achievements are too numerous to list, but some of the greater ones are worthy of mention. He has won the great classic, the Derby no less than eight times, a record no other jockey has ever approached. He has also won the *L'Arc de Triomph* three times; the Oaks, the Two Thousand Guineas, the St Leger and the Irish Sweeps Derby; in fact there is no great race that Lester has not won. The ever-present problem of so tall a man being able to make the weights has meant that he has had to pick his rides carefully, not accepting those with too low a weight. Lester has now been at the top of the tree for over thirty years, a remarkable record for any jockey, let alone one who has had to deny himself to keep his figure. How much longer we shall be privileged to see him riding winners nobody knows, but the day that Lester hangs up his boots will be all the poorer for the racing public.

### Richard Meade

Richard Meade must be one of the most experienced three-day event riders in the world. He has the distinction of having ridden in no less than four Olympic Games, during which he has won three Olympic Gold Medals.

Born in 1939, into a riding family, Richard's parents are former joint-masters of the Curre Hounds in Monmouthshire where they ran a Connemara pony stud. Unlike many international riders, Richard is not able to devote most of his time to riding and training. He was commissioned into the 11th Hussars before studying engineering at Cambridge and he is now a business consultant in London so riding has to be fitted in around his business life.

Lester Piggott.

Richard Meade.

**Hans Gunter Winkler**
Born on 24 July 1926, Hans did not take up jumping until after the Second World War, competing in his first adult competition in 1948 when he was twenty-two years old. He made his international debut in 1952, since when he has an outstanding record as an international rider, having won five Olympic gold medals, more than any other rider, and competed in over a hundred Nations Cups. His victories are many; they also include two World Championships and one European Championship. He has won Britain's King George V Cup twice, and has also helped many of Germany's young riders.

## Places

**The Spanish Riding School in Vienna**
When talking about famous places connected with horses, the Spanish Riding School in Vienna must come top of the list. It is the oldest riding establishment in the world, some type of school having been in existence there as early as 1572, although the magnificent riding school that we know today was opened in 1735.

Why an establishment in Austria should be so called needs some explanation. During the fifteenth and sixteenth centuries, the royal courts favoured the Spanish horses that were descended from Arab and Barb stallions and Andalusian mares.

Archduke Charles II founded a stud on part of his kingdom at Lipizza near Trieste, formerly in Austria, now in Yugoslavia. The land was very sparse, with very little vegetation and great expanses of bare rocks, but it was an area known to have been used for raising horses since Roman times. The first 'Hispanic' horses were imported, nine stallions and twenty-four mares.

The stud at Lipizza supplied horses to the court stables in Vienna – hence the name 'The Spanish Riding School' evolved. These horses bred at Lipizza became known as Lipizzaners, and it is these horses which are used exclusively in the school in Vienna.

The splendid buildings in the very heart of Vienna which were constructed for the riding school in the reign of Emperor Charles VI were the property of the court.

The purpose of the school was to preserve the equestrian art in its most noble form – high-school riding – which is still faithfully followed today. Young noblemen were instructed in the classic art of equitation, and the performances of the powerful stallions were highlights in court life.

The main aim of the school is to train instructors, who will then pass on their knowledge to other pupils. The school accepts a few foreign pupils each year; most of them stay for a year, during which time they will have the opportunity to reach a very high standard of horsemanship. The emphasis is placed on the whole art of riding, to be developed in three stages. Firstly, a style is developed in the most natural position where free forward movement is required, a stage that any competent rider can achieve. The second stage requires the rider to ride with a collected horse in perfect balance at all paces. Thirdly, the rider progresses to the more collected stage, when the horse has highly flexible joints showing great agility in the normal paces, and some of the more unusual movements including various jumps. This type of riding is called *haute école*.

# Horses

### Arkle

Arkle, owned by the Duchess of Westminster and trained by Tom Dreaper, was foaled on 19 April 1957, and is remembered today as one of the greatest steeplechasers ever to grace a racecourse.

A bronze statue of Arkle has been erected by his followers at Cheltenham, where he looks out across the course where he will be long remembered for his great exploits. It was here, as a five-year-old, that Arkle ran his first steeplechase and set a pattern by storming home to win by twenty lengths.

Arkle won many races, including the Cheltenham Gold Cup no less than three times. His racing career came to an end during the King George VI Cup race in 1967, when he cracked the pedal bone in one of his front feet. He spent three happy years in retirement, before being put to sleep in May 1970.

Arkle, who in thirty-five outings was unplaced only once, is seen here with his owner, the Duchess of Westminster.

### Red Rum

The story of Red Rum, who made history by winning the Grand National three times, is an amazing one.

During his first season's racing as a two-year-old, Red Rum was subjected to eight races with seven different jockeys, all of them hard ones, winning once more at Warwick – far from the ideal upbringing for a steeplechasing horse!

*Opposite*: Probably the most highly trained horses in the world, one of the Spanish Riding School's Lipizzaner stallions perform the *piaffe*. Equestrian statues are frequently of horses performing this movement.

Red Rum (in front) exercising on the shore at Southport, Lancashire.

As a three-year-old Red Rum had another hard season, progressing to the next stage of his career, hurdling. Once again he was unlucky enough to have several different jockeys, so that by the end of his first two years' racing he had been ridden by no less than fourteen jockeys. At the end of the season he won three more races in a row, ridden by Paddy Broderick.

In 1969 many stables were badly affected by the highly infectious 'cough'; and 'Rummy', as he was affectionately known, was no exception. The longstanding consequences were probably not appreciated and he was run no less than fourteen times, failing to win and only being placed three times; this with yet another string of jockeys that brought the total now to twenty.

The next year he was schooled over fences and then began the third stage of his racing career – National Hunt Racing. He had thirteen races, ridden by Tommy Stack in most of them, winning three. The following season saw several changes in Red Rum's management, with the retirement of Bobby Renton and subsequent taking over by Tommy Stack and then by Anthony Gillam. Red Rum also developed foot trouble, in spite of which he gallantly ran in several more races, winning one of them. Then he was lame for two months with a foot condition that is usually incurable; due to the care taken by Anthony Gillam and the help of the best treatment that could be obtained, he made a slow recovery and was gently got fit for the next season when he ran in the Scottish National, finishing fifth. When Mrs Brotherton cut down the numbers of her horses, Red Rum was one of the three horses to be sold.

Bought by Ginger McCain for Mr Noel Le Mare for 6,000 guineas,

Red Rum was sold for the last time at public auction. Ginger was a second-hand car salesman who trained a few horses he kept in a back yard behind his business in Southport. With no gallops to use he had to train his horses on the sands. The therapeutic effect of the sea, and the lack of jarring on the roads seemed to be just the answer to Rummy's problems. Under Ginger's regime he won his first six races in a row, then was given a rest before preparing him for the 1973 Grand National. He was only placed in his next three races, then came the big one, when Brian Fletcher was selected to ride him.

The Australian horse Crisp was top weight that year, carrying 12 stone (76.2 kg). Crisp led by ten lengths over the last fence with Red Rum lying second; on the long run in the extra weight proved too much for Crisp and Red Rum passed him to win the first National he had run in, and break the time record set by Golden Miller. The welcome for the local hero was jubilant and the name McCain became a household word.

Red Rum had well earned his summer's rest; when he came back into work he seemed none the worse for the tough race at Aintree. He ran in a few more races but the main aim was for the Grand National again. In 1974 he was given top weight, the ground dried out in time to suit him and he ran a remarkable race, leading from Bechers Brook the second time round and winning easily by seven lengths. The crowd went mad with excitement; there was no doubt that Red Rum thoroughly deserved his second victory.

Amid much criticism Ginger decided to run him three weeks later in the Scottish National at Ayr. The great horse created racing history by winning both Nationals in the same year, and a year later a bronze statue of him was unveiled before the start of the Scottish National.

The Grand National still remained the target for Red Rum; Aintree was regarded as 'his course'. He had already equalled the previous record of winning twice, but more was to come. In 1975 he ran again, but this time the first two placings were reversed with L'Escargot taking the victor's crown. Red Rum again ran in the Scottish National, but with only two weeks between the races he was not up to his old form and was beaten once more.

In 1976 Red Rum ran for the fourth time in the National, this time finishing second to Rag Trade. What a record, two wins and twice second! In 1977 he was back yet again on his favourite course at Aintree and then he really did make history. He won his third Grand National and received the greatest ovation any horse could from the jubilant crowd. There was hardly a dry eye there as this fantastic horse stormed home in the lead once more. The following year Red Rum was prepared to run again but just before the race he bruised a heel and had to be withdrawn. He paraded down the course, showing his disgust at being unable to run by bucking and kicking and generally showing-off. After this he was retired from racing, but he keeps a very full appointment book with numerous engagements to parade at shows and other functions. 'Rummy' is probably the most courageous racehorse we shall ever see, who succeeded in spite of disadvantages he had to cope with, and whose record is unlikely to be broken or even equalled.

# *Index*

*Page numbers in italic refer to illustrations*